For Such a Time as This

Re-Imaging Practical Theology for Independent Pentecostal Churches

Antipas L. Harris

The Asbury Theological Seminary Series in
World Christian Revitalization Movements in Pentecostal/Charismatic Studies,
No. 1

EMETH PRESS
www.emethpress.com

For Such a Time as This,
Re-Imaging Practical Theology for Independent Pentecostal Churches

Copyright © 2010 Antipas L Harris
Printed in the United States of America on acid-free paper

All rights reserved. No part of this book may be reproduced, or stored in a retrieval system or transmitted in any form or by any means, electronic, mechanical, photocopying, recording, scanning or otherwise, except as permitted by the 1976 United States Copyright Act, or with the prior written permission of Emeth Press. Requests for permission should be addressed to: Emeth Press, P. O. Box 23961, Lexington, KY 40523-3961.
http://www.emethpress.com.

Library of Congress Cataloging-in-Publication Data.
Harris, Antipas L.
 For such a time as this : re-imaging practical theology for independent Pentecostal churches / Antipas L. Harris.
   p. cm. -- (Asbury Theological Seminary series in world Christian revitalization movements)
 Includes bibliographical references (p.   ) and index.
 ISBN 978-1-60947-000-5 (alk. paper)
 1. African American Pentecostal churches--Government. 2. Independent churches--United States--Government. 3. African American Pentecostal churches--Doctrines. 4. Independent churches--United States--Doctrines. 5. Christianity and culture--United States. 6. Theology, Practical--United States. I. Title.
 BX8762.5.Z5H37 2010
 262'.099408996073--dc22
                               2010002354

Dedication

This Book is Dedicated in the
Love and Memory of my Grandmother
(Mrs. Elsie Parks)
and
My Grandfather
(Mr. Jack Amos Parks)

Contents

Foreword	9
Preface	13
Acknowledgements	15
Chapter 1: Introduction	17
Chapter 2: Independent Pentecostal Churchs: Ramifications	23
Chapter 3: Culture: Theological Criterion or Theological Enemy?	37
Chapter 4: The Ordination of Women	62
Chapter 5: A Proposal: The Trilateral Paradigm in the Life of the Church	81
Bibliography	97
Index	111

8

Foreword

The twentieth century has witnessed a new form of Christianity quite distinct from the historic denominations. A large segment of the rapidly growing movements in the Global South is 'independent', sometimes described as *'churches of the Spirit'*. This phenomenal growth is characterized by a great diversity of cultural and religious expressions, as people interpret the Bible from their own contexts and their particular worldview and speak for themselves. Human beings suffering from predicaments, discrimination and poverty search for images and symbols that give meaning to their lives, create order and promise redemption in the transition from death to life. Many western churches and theologies continue to regard this development as schismatic, meaning an aberration from the norms of traditional Christianity. Because these movements originated among Africans, Asians, Blacks in the Caribbean, or for that matter among African Americans, they are often dismissed in terms like "sectarian" or "separatist." Yet, current trends suggest that this mobilization at the grassroots of communities will be the driving force of Christian mission in post-modern times, with all promises and risks.

Antipas Harris' examination of independent pentecostal-type churches in the United States is timely as he searches for the theological criteria under which movements like these can become vehicles for the revitalization of the Christian church. The two churches under investigation, as part of the African American 'churches of the Spirit', are with rather extreme doctrines, and practices not even the best models for renewal. However, they serve as telling examples that those claiming to actively rely on the power of the Holy Spirit can still remain inflexible and complicit in their own oppression. Under which conditions, he asks, will their 'independent' approach produce a practical theology that is liberating and a mirror of the love of Christ in living contexts? In other words, can there be a re-imaging of ecclesiology, sound leadership and critical practices?

To illustrate his enquiry, the author has chosen (in place of other burning issues such as social politics, climate change or homosexuality) conflicts relating to *gender,* both the leadership and ordination of women, and their restricted dress code in black pentecostal-type congregations. As 'trivial' as the latter observance might be, it illustrates how practical issues like this relate to much deeper theological underpinnings which hinder the transformation of oppressive practices. Hence, as a counter-framework and guide, he develops what he calls the *Trilateral* paradigm in the life of the church, namely the indispensable interplay between Scripture, experiences of the Holy Spirit, and culture - a hermeneutic tool for avoiding both mis-readings of the Bible, and the lack of cultural critique and of cultural affirmation (here in the context of the struggle of African

Americans for justice in a white society). I feel reminded of Emil Brunner's concept of *'encounter'* as the breaking-in of God's Spirit into our human conditions. Liberation theology speaks of *text and context*, the fact that the Bible is the binding resource for the church, but so is the response to people's needs - real people in diverse cultural settings.

By introducing the concept of *culture*, the book contributes constructively to the ongoing debate how the development of Biblical interpretation and Christian doctrine (by no means in pentecostalism only!) has been shaped by culture, or by diverse cultural, Religious, and social contexts in which Christ's message has taken roots. The inability of Christians as a whole to critically engage culture in making theological judgments has resulted in the western confusion of the gospel with a specific culture, Eurocentrism, and ensuing domineering structures. There is an urgent need for re-interpreting Scripture in the light of altered cultural norms and consequently for reshaping congregational practices. Lamin Sanneh calls this the ongoing *translatability of the gospel*, Christianity's capacity for cross-cultural transmission or cross-cultural transplantation, expressing itself in multiple patterns and fluent alliances. Hence, instead of using the (Catholic) term of 'inculturation', I prefer to speak of indigenization and contextualization.

Antipas himself has been raised in a pentecostal-holiness tradition, and has degrees in music (as cultural expression) and in New Testament. Thus, he is uniquely equipped for such an analysis of the ongoing interaction between *kerygma* and culture both in the Bible and in independent Christian movements. He conjures up a theological vision of cultural affirmation as well as cultural critique for reshaping doctrine and practice in congregations; otherwise they become "theologically dry, paranoid and judgmental of cultural nuances that differ from one group to another." The reason why pentecostalism spreads globally is its capacity to take shape in diverse milieus, adapting, affirming and challenging culture, enabling people anywhere to indigenize the gospel in their particular contexts and express the Christian faith in their own modes of communication.

Consequently, pastors of independent churches need formal training in biblical criticism and should have access to viable education programs in the areas of biblical studies, spirituality, and cultural anthropology. I am reminded of various Theological Education by Extension (TEE) programs in the Global South, but even more so of our own endeavor at the Centre for Black and White Christian Partnership in Birmingham, UK. It introduced, thirty years ago, pastors of African and Caribbean independent churches in Britain to a leadership training based on Biblical studies, Christian doctrine and an intercultural understanding of Mission. It took its methods from Paulo Freire's *'pedagogy of the oppressed'* transferred into the situation of a multiracial society in Europe. It did away with the traditional teacher/student or subject/object paradigm, made everybody an 'expert' in his or her own tradition, laid the responsibility for running such a project into the joint hands of staff and participants, and introduced prayer and worship as equally valid educational experiences. In this way, it equipped Christians in the urban cities for power-sharing and a joint mission in a segregated and disjointed society. This responds to Thomas Groome's community-based educational program suggested here: i.e. *participation, partnership and dialogue,* as a paradigm for *shared* praxis, communal insights and liberating togetherness. In the conclusion, I would have wished for some practical outline of strategies how to achieve this aim, perhaps in response to earlier projects such as in Rochester (Wilmore) decades ago - material for another book?

A last observation: I credit Harris in his effort to emphasize female liberation in the church, but I do not agree that the exclusion of women from the ministry is mainly due to Eurocentric influence. Inasmuch there exists an alternative tradition of women's emancipation in western thought, inasmuch there is also the unbroken dominance of patriarchy in African societies, challenged by the 'Circle for Concerned African Women Theologians', and by Womanism in Black theology in America. The issue of the liberation of women from oppression, long challenged by Christ's Gospel, lies still underneath all societies.

Dr. Roswith Gerloff, Potsdam,
8.August 2009

Preface

I was born into a Spirit-filled family and raised in a traditional, independent pentecostal-holiness church. As a child, my vision of Christianity was shaped by very fundamental pentecostal-holiness ideology and theology. This tradition nurtured me in its understanding of Christianity and taught me what it means to be born-again and filled with the "Holy Ghost" (with initial evidence of speaking in tongues). My love for the church remains as I also answered my call to ministry from those very pews. Over the years, I have come to appreciate how my Christian heritage has shaped my thinking and laid the foundation for my critical theological reflections.

Because of my religious background, for example, I can agree with scholars, i.e., historians, sociologists, and theologians, who assert that the pentecostal and holiness movements impacted the spread of global evangelism in dialogue with "World Christianity."[1] One outcome of global evangelism is that near the end of the twentieth century, some theological academies had expanded their curricula to include the study of pentecostalism including the independent pentecostal churches.

Among the growing number of scholars who identify themselves with the pentecostal-type heritage, several focus their studies on such churches in the African Diaspora. Among these is a small number of African American scholars who are practical theologians. Given the paucity of research studies – experiential and otherwise – within this evolving field, my research will help to establish a foundation for the study of pentecostal-type churches within practical theology, as well as for broader-based African American theological scholarship.

I intend to conduct a study using a praxis[2]-related theological framework, to explore the possibilities of a reshaped theological paradigm within independent pentecostal-type churches. My goal is to help these churches wrestle critically with theological judgments, biblical hermeneutics, and ecclesial practices in order to produce doctrinal practices more reflective of the liberating nature of the gospel. This book is praxis-related in that it focuses on issues that emerge more specifically from congregational practices and lifts those concerns critical reflection. The objective is to return to practice with recommendations for reformed ecclesial practices. The significance of this work rests in its potential to re-image theological traditions and to develop strategies for transforming independent pentecostal church practices.

As an insider, in my observation of independent pentecostal-type churches of the African Diaspora, there is a high level of sensitivity towards the importance of Scripture, the gifts and experiences of the Holy Spirit, and culture. Yet, the treatment of these tenets for theological and ecclesial doctrinal judgment seems to produce the problem of non-critical, contradictory or exclusionary doctrinal practices. It is relevant to the field of practical theology to examine these tenets with a view towards re-imaging ecclesiology for more critical church practices.

Upon joining the faculty at Regent University School of Divinity, I have been intrigued with the focus here on "Renewal Studies." I have therefore, adapted "Renewal Studies" as part of my Practical Theological research. This book is, moreover, my contribution to the academic conversations surrounding "Renewal Studies," in language accessible to pastors and church leaders. Within a practical theological framework, my question is "what does 'Renewal Studies' mean in light of practical theology of ministry within independent pentecostal churches?" As result of my quest, I have changed the title of this book as, coincidentally, my doctoral research prior to joining Regent faculty has lead me to a preliminary response to that very question. Therefore, the current title is not a square peg forced in the round hole.

Notes

1. Examples include Allan H. Anderson, *An Introduction to Pentecostalism: Global Charismatic Christianity* (United Kingdom: University of Cambridge, 2004), Harvey Cox, *Fire from Heaven: The Rise of Pentecostalism and Reshaping of Religion in the Twenty-First Century* (Da Capo Press, 1995), David Martin, *Pentecostalism: The World Their Parish* (Malden, MA: Blackwell Publishers, 2002), and Vinson Synan, *The Holiness-Pentecostal Tradition: Charismatic Movements of the Twentieth Century* (Grand Rapids: William B. Eerdmans Publishing Co, 1997).

2. Some scholars, such as mission scholar K. C. Abraham, define *praxis* with a focus on the need for critical reflection on historical, as well as contemporary, experience as relevant theological education. Other scholars, such as Don Browning, define *praxis* as critical reflections that begin in practice, then move to theory and then return to practice with strategic proposals for reshaped or transformed practice in light of critical reflections (See the "Definitions" section for reference information). My definition of *praxis* draws from Don Browning's *practice-theology-practice* formula, which begins in practice, moves to critical theoretical or theological reflections, and returns to practice with strategic proposals for reshaped doctrinal practices.

Acknowledgments

There are so many people to acknowledge and thank. First of all, I thank God and my Lord and Savior Jesus Christ who has made my success possible! I thank God for being gracious, loving and forgiving, and for the strength to make it this far.

I am indebted to the editors and subeditors of the Asbury Theological Seminary Series in Christian Revitalization, the Pentecostal and Charismatic Studies Series within which this monograph finds itself. I am grateful to the Center for the Study of World Christian Revitalization Movements at Asbury, Dr. Bill Faupel and Dr. Steve O'Malley and as well as Dr. Larry Wood of Emeth Academic Press. These men are gracious to helpful in choosing this book to publish as part of this series. I am also thankful to Dr. Amos Yong, a fellow-alumnus of Boston University, colleague at Regent University and good friend. His constructive genius continues to challenge my scholarship and to help me navigate the divine paths set for me in theological education and academic ministry. I have Amos to thank for introducing me to Dr. Faupel for consideration in this current series.

I wish to thank my parents –Pastor James L. and Lady Carolyn J. Harris -- for their many prayers and support throughout my college career. Also, I want to extend very special thanks to several persons who have helped to nurture me personally, spiritually and academically. I am grateful for my "supervisors" (teachers) at Christian Way Academy, Sis. Jenie E. Carter, Sis. Ruth Purnell, and the late Sis. Tamara Buchanan, who each believed in my scholarship potential when I was only a young boy.

This book began as my dissertation that bore the title: *Re-Envisioning Independent Pentecostal-type Ecclesiology for the Twenty-first Century: Considerations from the African Christian Diaspora.* I thank my helpful and gracious doctoral advisors at Boston University School of Theology, Dr. Dale P. Andrews and Dean John H. Berthrong. I want to thank Dr. Andrews for not objecting to my creative ideas and for spending so much time helping me to think critically and organize my thoughts on paper. I thank Dean Berthrong for his support and for believing that this particular project is an important one for the theological academy. I am convinced that divine providence orchestrated that I work with these advisors. Therefore, I extend my deepest thanks to God for them. They spent so much time guiding, and encouraging me, reading and re-reading my drafts, and helping me to develop my scholarship. Drs. Andrews and Berthrong were more than advisors; they were academic mentors and friends. In addition to my advisors, I would like to extend hearty thanks to two other members of my dissertation committee --Dr. John Hart and Dr. James C. Walters. Their critique of my dissertation proposal was extremely helpful, and crucial to the preliminary revision of it towards the production of this monograph.

Furthermore, I would like to thank the Rev. Dr. Monifa A. Jumanne for the countless hours she spent reading my manuscript and providing grammatical edits. Without her, I could not have produced this document in its current form. In addition, I would like to thank my brother ---Norman Andronicus Harris --- and my good friend – Thurmon Knox -- for taking time from their busy schedule to critique my work. I extend special thanks to my graduate assistants at Regent University School of Theology—Rachel Santiago and Adria Jenkins-Jones, my sister --Naomi L. Harris-Hines, and The Reverend Charrise Barron for their proofreading skills.

I am deeply indebted to several scholars who took the time to read my work and offer helpful feedback. My long-time academic mentor, and dearest friend, the Rev. Dr. Roswith Gerloff of the University of Leeds in England and Founder of the Centre for Black and White Christian Partnership in Birmingham, England, has supported me and contributed extremely helpful critique of my manuscript, advancing it towards its current draft. I can always count on Dr. Gerloff's candid critiques, constructive suggestions, and tireless motivation when I need it most. Dr. Harvey Cox has been nothing short of inspiration and encouragement since I took a reading course on "Pentecostal Theology" with him at Harvard during the spring of 2003. He challenged me to think about theological paradigms among independent pentecostal churches and the trajectories set among them towards the future of the pentecostal movement. The Rev. Dr. Michael J. Brown of Emory University has been a supportive friend since 1999 when I was a student at Candler School of Theology. Brown provided helpful critique of this manuscript as well. Dr. Dana Robert of Boston University has been a supportive academic force who has helped me think critically and intently about my academic journey and the value of strong scholarship. The Rev. Dr. Brad Ronnell Braxton has been a source of moral support in my academic journey until now. His scholarship has been inspiration, as I also combine academic scholarship and academic ministry with practical ministry. I must, also, acknowledge that there are countless others to acknowledge for their significant contributions along my academic journey. However, time and space will neither permit more names nor allow me to explain all the ways these individuals have helped me in my academic pursuits. Words are inadequate to express my sincere gratitude for all their many expressions of support, guidance, and encouragement

Chapter 1

Introduction

I approach this task with questions about the gifts, experiences, and culture of the Holy Spirit in the formation and development of independent pentecostal-type churches[1] of the African Diaspora.[2] The core problem is that there is a breakdown in the relationship between (mis)interpretations of scripture, experiences of the Holy Spirit and perceptions of culture (the lack of intentional inclusion of culture and/or the misuse of cultural elements)—what I call the "trilateral." The pages ahead explain how this "trilateral relationship" of scripture, workings of the Holy Spirit and culture are important to the viability of the churches and should come together, affirming the liberating power of the gospel of Jesus Christ. The bulk of my illustrations emerge from a core theological problem present among some African American independent pentecostal churches today.

In most urban cities across America such as Boston, Washington D.C., Chicago, Atlanta, New Haven, Newark, and Los Angeles, independent pentecostal-type churches appear to be on nearly every corner. They are also in increasing saturation around the world for example in Porte-Au-Prince, Kingston, Kinshasa, Buenos Aire, Lima, Seoul, Johannesburg, Paris, Berlin and among many of the underground churches in China. Some are denominationally affiliated, but maintain a level of ecclesial autonomy on the local level. Several of them have separated from traditional denominations. The separated churches do not look to denominational hierarchy for ecclesial structure or guidance when making theological judgments. Throughout these pages, I use the terms "independent pentecostal churches" and "independent pentecostal-type churches" interchangeably. You will notice that throughout this book the word "Pentecostal" begins with a lower-case "p." I am borrowing this from scholars like Allen Anderson and Roswith Gerloff who use the lower-case "p" in their efforts to speak to the emerging independent churches that value the move of the Holy Spirit but are not part of traditional western Pentecostal denominations, nor do they trace their origin directly to the American pentecostal movement of the early twentieth century. These churches are primarily independent and in many cases indigenous. As indigenous churches, many of these churches, globally, do not have direct affiliations to western mission churches. I believe that this book is helpful for both the independent pentecostal-type churches with denominational antecedents as well as global indigenous churches. Both of these categories must evaluate their theological systems for making theological judgment in church practice to contend for application amidst critical thinking of this century.

As independent pentecostal or pentecostal-type churches expand globally, they give rise to a growing concern with particular practices, methods of theological interpretation, and doctrine. These churches place a high value on Scripture, experiences of the Holy Spirit, and culture in making theological judgments regarding doctrinal practices. Yet, there are increasing inconsistencies in the ways these three criteria are applied in determining those judgments for church practice.

Inconsistencies in theological matters often generate conflicting claims in Scriptural interpretations, the Holy Spirit's revelations, and cultural perceptions. Denominational polity and theological rationales for certain church practices are often unilateral judgments of a single pastor and often oppressive to women. The former (unilateral leadership on theological matters) is inconsistent with the scriptural model of leadership for theological judgment in Acts 15th chapter, wherein there is a council of Elders at Jerusalem that deliberates over circumcision to determine a viable church practice consistent with the role of the Holy Spirit sent to represent the risen Lord. The latter (gender oppression) is inconsistent with the liberating nature of the gospel as expressed in Luke 8:18 and the teachings of Paul regarding the gender and ethnic inclusive gospel message in, for example, such as in Galatians 3:28.

A critical example, hotly debated, is that women are often not allowed to preach. This seems to be an impasse that frequently emerges between authoritative claims on revelations of the Holy Spirit and interpretations of Scripture. Women often claim spiritual experiences wherein God calls them to preach. However, many of them are constrained by traditional interpretations of scripture that prohibit them from pursuing what they claim that the Spirit has charged them to do. Such stalemates surface not only with reference to women's ordination, but also at times to lay participation in worship and church ministries.

Another critical example is the practice, stemming from doctrine, of restricting women from wearing pants or trousers. Such teaching reveals the inordinate repression or misuse of cultural elements in consideration of limited insight or theological reflection on selected passages of Scripture. As such, it illustrates a deep paradigmatic problem amongst the relationship between biblical, spiritual and cultural theological developments, and as they relate to church practices among many pentecostal-type churches. I will return to further develop these discussions in the following pages.

I employ methods of practical theology to explore two fundamental cases affecting women's roles in pentecostal-type churches. These cases demonstrate dominant patterns in the impasse between church practices and theological doctrine that shape ecclesial identity. I search for a reformulation of pentecostal-type ecclesiology that will engage Scripture, theological traditions, and contemporary cultural contexts for the activity and revelation of the Holy Spirit. In this pursuit, I submit a critical treatment of a trilateral paradigm consisting of 1) Scripture, 2) experiences of the Holy Spirit, and 3) culture, in making critical, coherent, and consistent theological judgments for pentecostal-type church practices.

The trilateral paradigm is used in two ways. The first is as a means of explaining the issues within church doctrinal practice that evolve from an uncritical application of the trilateral. Using the trilateral, I reflect on a few examples of church practices which might draw attention to the need for a more rigorous theological process. These cases both illustrate and address the historic and continuing impasse between articulate theological doctrine and consistent church practices within a broader endeavor to shape (or reshape) pentecostal-type ecclesiology. Secondly, a critical reformulation of the trilateral becomes the locus of systematic theology within the practical theological enterprise. In this movement, the critical trilateral paradigm becomes a transient moment between practical interests and subsequent strategic proposals for a reshaped practice.

A relevant resource for theological reflection on church practices is the *African Christian Diaspora Conference* which took place in Berlin in 2003.[3] This conference involved bishops, pastors, theologians, and other scholars from pentecostal-type traditions of the African Diaspora and included hotly debated discourse on women and ministry. The examples test my proposed trilateral model (Scripture, experiences of the Holy Spirit and culture) for its effectiveness in producing theologically strong practices for the church and ecclesial doctrine.

The following questions will guide my exploration of these cases: 1) How does Scripture support church practices regarding "holy attire" that, for example, prohibit women from wearing pants in church? 2) How shall we re-interpret certain scriptural passages such that they affirm gender equality in the governance of the church through ordained ministry? Scripture is consistently used to affirm certain cultural practices, including styles of dress, while other cultural practices that seem contrary to the gospel escape such theological scrutiny.

The central focus of this project can be distilled into the following question: How do we engage theological tenets relevant to doctrinal practices of independent pentecostal-type churches (interpretations of Scripture, revelations of the Holy Spirit and perceptions of culture) in a manner that will help to make sound judgments for doctrinal practices in a re-envisioned ecclesiology? The following sub-questions will help guide the exploration of this central question:

1. How have ministers with limited formal theological training and little ministerial leadership training, shaped the theological and ministerial leadership of pentecostal-type churches in the African Diaspora?

2. What is the role of the Holy Spirit in shaping or reshaping ecclesiology?

3. Should there be a theological relationship between interpretations of Scripture, experiences of the Holy Spirit, and perceptions of culture in a reshaped ecclesiology that might help to reshape doctrinal practices considered oppressive and exclusive (based on gender) to believers within the church?

4. Are there examples of ordained women ministers in twentieth century pentecostalism that might serve as examples of women preachers effective in the

spread of pentecostalism? How might their roles support the need for a reshaping of pentecostal-type ecclesiology as proposed here?

5. What proposition for Christian education would help independent pentecostal-type churches critically reshape doctrinal practices in order to minimize risks related to the current execution of the trilateral model: interpretations of Scripture, experiences of the Holy Spirit and perceptions of culture?

In addressing these questions this volume generates alternate possibilities for reshaping pentecostal-type ecclesiology that wrestle with revelation and culture. The challenge will be in forming methods for shaping and reshaping church practices that do not compromise core theological tenets of these churches, yet remain open to redefining the church's identity and mission in the world.

This study will reveal how the tenets of the trilateral (Scripture, experiences of the Holy Spirit and culture) form a complex relationship. While these tenets are valued as important to re-envisioning doctrinal polity and ecclesial practices, they are often not critically engaged by contemporary church leadership. Consequently, the doctrinal practices determined thereafter may not be consistent with the liberating nature of the gospel. Some non-critical treatment of these theological tenets has resulted in exclusionary practices in ministerial ordination that contradict the important leadership, even pastoral roles that women assume in the development of particular congregations, as well as in the spiritual growth of the church. These doctrinal interpretations sometimes even exclude themselves from fellowship with other Christian churches with ordained female leadership.

Conflicts between theological tenets and doctrine often pose challenges when, for example, the interpretation of Scripture excludes women from preaching or from carrying out pastoral ministry. However, women within these churches appeal to the tradition's theological doctrines of the Holy Spirit and contend that the Holy Spirit has revealed to them, either by religious experience or through a spiritual gift, the calling of God on their lives to preach or to serve in pastoral ministry. Both Scripture and the Holy Spirit are tenets of esteemed value among independent pentecostal churches. Yet, it appears that sometimes, in ecclesial practices, one of the theological tenets may actually cancel or preempt another. This dynamic cannot be narrowly relegated to claims made by women seeking ministerial leadership in the church. The conflict is lodged among the theological tenets themselves, and is best evidenced by ecclesial practices. I contend, therefore, that if all the tenets are to remain theologically authoritative within these churches, there must be a more critical, more productive means of binding the tenets together to transform ostensibly oppressive practices. This would allow for the creation of theological judgments consistent with ecclesial identity, mission, and practices.

It is all too easy to misconstrue my purpose in this book. The emphasis is profoundly critical of the churches under consideration in order to develop my focus. However, my analysis should not communicate that there is no good in these churches. The first example, the Church of God, Pillar of Truth Church has done a lot of good for the youth in their church. Particularly, their parochial school has a history of graduating respectable and intelligent young men and women who are now contributing much to society as they each serve the communities within which they each live. Second, the Rock of Life Church should also be acknowledged for its contribution to the development of urban youth through after school programs and empowerment sessions. In all fairness, these churches have many other positive contributions, for example, focusing on the preservation and development of healthy family life, highlighting the importance of spiritual development and the role of the church in making these successes possible. Treatment of these and other positive contributions should be addressed in greater depth in another book.

However, there is an increasing demand, particularly from the people in the pews, for critical and coherent ecclesiology and practical teachings; therefore, there is a hunger for strong practical theological methods. These methods would embrace the plausible successes of these ministries while at the same time providing stronger theological foundation for their church doctrine and potential means for transforming ecclesial identity, mission, and practices.

Notes

1. Allan H. Anderson, "Challenges and Prospects for Research into AICs in Southern Africa," Paper read at the Centre for the Study of Christianity in the Non-Western World, University of Edinburgh, January 1996, *Missionalia* 23:3, November 1995 (283-284); http://artsweb.bham.ac.uk/aanderson/Publications/challenges_and_prospects_for_res.htm (accessed 21 December 2007). Anderson uses the term "Pentecostal-type" to refer to those AICs in Southern Africa which have their origins in the healing and Pentecostal movements at the beginning of the twentieth century. These churches are usually (but not always) called "Zionist" churches or "Apostolic" churches. These churches were influenced by the North American Classical Pentecostal churches but are not a part of those denominations and do not fully (if at all) subscribe to their doctrinal teachings. I have adapted this term to the "charismatic" or "Spirit-filled" churches of the twenty-first century (independent and alliance churches) that include speaking in tongues and prophesying as central elements of baptism of the Spirit and the communal worship experience.

2. The term "African Christian Diaspora" refers to congregations located geographically outside the continent of Africa. These congregations are comprised of African-descended persons and tend to be led by pastors of African descent. The term also refers to congregations that value expressions of worship that trace their roots to the African continent.

3. *The Third International Interdisciplinary Conference of the African Christian Diaspora* took place under the title "The Berlin-Congo Conference 1884, the Partition of Africa, and Implications for Christian Mission Today", in September 2003. It was organized by Roswith Gerloff, Afe Adogame, and Klaus Hock under the auspices of Humboldt University, Berlin, Rostock University, and the Academy of Mission at Hamburg University, Germany – in cooperation with the Council of Christian Communities of an African Approach in Europe. Its findings have been published under the title *The Shaping of Christianity in Africa and the African Diaspora* (London: Continuum, 2008).

Chapter 2

Independent Pentecostal Churches: Ramifications

Situation of Independent Pentecostal Churches

As indicated in the previous chapter, scholars and church leaders refer to what I call independent pentecostal or pentecostal-type churches with various terms. Some call them independent churches of the Spirit, independent Spirit-filled churches, independent neocharismatic churches, independent postdenominational churches. David Barrett and Todd M. Johnson summarize the many names among what I have defined as "independent pentecostal-type churches" under the category of "Third Wave Neocharismatic Renewal."[1]

In his article "Three Waves of Christian Renewal," Johnson surveys three waves of Christian renewal over the last one hundred years.[2] Then he projects the numbers for 2025. Members of the renewal survey include Africa, North America, Asia, Europe, Latin America and Oceana. In 2006, the record showed in these areas a total population of 6,529,426,000. Of this more than 6 billion people, 2,156,350,000 were Christians. 596,096,000 were Renewalist Christians. This number is 27.6% of total global Christians compared to 0.2% of global Christians in 1906. Johnson's projections reveal that in 2025, of a total global population of 7,851,455,000, there will be 2,630,559,000 total numbers of Christians. By 2025, the total projected number of renewalists will be 789,320,000, which is 30% of the total number of Christians then. From 1906 to now, the annual percentage rate of "First and Second Wave Renewal Christians" has decreased. Johnson's projections show that over the next nineteen years, the "First Wave Pentecostal Renewal Christians" (including classical pentecostals, denominational pentecostals etc) will increase at no more than 1.0% rate per year. The Second Wave Charismatic Renewal Christians (including mostly denominational charismatic churches, etc) would increase at no more than a 2.4% rate per year. But the "Third Wave Renewal Christians" (including the independent Pentecostals, neocharismatics, etc) would increase by up to 4.0% per year. The record projects that the global numbers of renewal Christians continue to rise annually in percentage of total Christians. Of the three waves of renewal Christians, the "Third Wave Renewalist Movement" is expected to increase more than the other two waves of renewal Christians by 2025. Some of the current independent churches involved in this "Third Wave Renewalist Movement" (or independent pentecostal-type churches) did not exist at the inception of the

"First Wave Renewalist Movement" (at the inception of classical pentecostals and denominational pentecostals) in 1906. However, in the twentieth century various sub-movements expanded a continuously reformed overarching pentecostal movement (e.g. First Wave and Second Wave Renewal Movements) and will continue to expand throughout the twenty-first century in record breaking rates through the "independent pentecostal churches," or "churches of the Spirit" of the Third Wave Renewalist Movement.

Seeing the growing number of independent pentecostal Christians, I am particularly concerned with their churches. I believe that there needs to be greater attention given to the move of the Spirit among the independent pentecostal congregations. Additionally, per my observation, there needs to be greater investigation into their theological framework, and places in their ecclesiastical structures and doctrinal constructions where they might strengthen for greater impact in the world and continued faithfulness to the mission of God in Christ and the moving of the Holy Spirit.

Practical Theological Question

Clear theological arbitration has remained the weakness in the ecclesial structures of pentecostal churches since the beginning of the American movement in the early nineteen hundreds. As Douglas Jacobsen rightly states, there has not been a "meta-model of pentecostalism-- no essence of pentecostalism of normative archetype-- that can provide an infallible rule against which to judge all the various particular renditions of pentecostal faith and theology."[3] As leaders emerged in the movement, their often unilateral and uncritical theological insights have frequently led them to doctrinal decisions for their congregations. Their followers, being exceedingly excited about their experience of Spirit baptism, time and again assimilated to the guidelines of their leadership.

Times are changing now. If these churches are to continue to draw young people, there is a need for deeper theological analysis and reformed ecclesiologies. Young people of the pentecostal pews have more and more critical questions about their faith. They want definitive theological reasoning before adapting to church practices. There must be clearer theological accountability -- even if on the level of the local churches-- to insure critical, non-oppressive church doctrine. This theology must be faithful to the liberating gospel of love and grace within a theological corpus that takes seriously Scripture, the Holy Spirit and perceptions of culture. The practical theological question is this: is there a way to assess the tenets of Scripture, revelations of the Holy Spirit, and culture, in order to make more consistent theological judgments for doctrinal practice in a re-envisioned ecclesiology? These three elements are all relevant to the doctrinal practices of independent pentecostal-type churches. The problem is that several practices are functionally antithetical to these theological tenets regarding certain (mis)interpretation of Scripture, experiences of the Holy Spirit and perceptions of culture.

In subsequent chapters, two questions guide the discussion of illustrations in this project. The first question is: How can we interpret certain Scriptural passages with reference to experiences of the Holy Spirit, such that there is stronger affirmation of gender inclusion in church governance, while simultaneously sustaining the centrality of Scripture in pentecostal doctrinal practice? The second question concerns the theological worldview of culture and the doctrinal practices in churches that propagate what is "holy." For example, pentecostal-type churches that prohibit women from wearing pants have developed theological or doctrinal tenets on "holy attire." Much of the discussion either for or against this issue seems theologically underdeveloped. In response, is there a way to understand the convergence of culture and Scripture that both affirms and critically analyzes the issue to generate a more theologically reflective practice?[4]

This chapter describes only a few doctrinal practices that illustrate the deeper theological problem presented in this book. I have chosen randomly to reflect on the accounts in this chapter. I conduct a systematic theological analysis of the dilemma in light of situations that emerge from two church examples. This book recommends re-imaging the formulation of doctrine in order to produce more critical, and theologically coherent doctrinal practices among independent pentecostal churches for the twenty-first century.

There are several other issues exemplary to the concern of robust theological framework among these churches. There are almost as many examples as there are independent churches. Some of these examples include questionable theologies pertaining to the practices of marriage, tithing, dress and church leadership. This chapter analyzes the ramifications of problematic theological frameworks. The contemporary global society, as more and more cultures are increasingly giving credence to women's voices, sheds light on the vital role women have always played in the formation of societies and Christian churches. This illumination also brings to light the horrific historical oppression women have endured in the church, even in the name of God.

The problem or problem among churches, as I see it, is a theological one because it results from certain mis-readings of biblical texts, coupled with biased cultural bindings of the past. Problematic examples of the deeper theological crisis easily observable are displayed in the "weak" theology and questionable doctrinal practices specific to the issues of 1) the ordination of women, and 2) "holy attire" for women. I refer to the theology as "weak" because the arguments supporting these practices seem to contradict the theological tenets central to these churches' own understanding of freedom and love in the pentecostal-type experience. Albeit rather superficial to contemporary thinkers, I have chosen some of the simpler but real arguments that result from the theological issue identified in these pages. The simple arguments are yet strong examples to expose the problem in weak church doctrine. The illustrations concerning "holy attire" and women in ministry represents a wider trend of competing claims on the theological tenets of Scripture, Holy Spirit and culture. I contend that the theological problem exposed in these pages represent the deep theological challenges among more complex theological issues such as marriage and re-marriage, homosexuality and same-sex marriage. Independent pentecostal churches would be in a better position to make sound theological arguments concerning these and other issues when they have a more intentional and rigorous theological framework by which they make doctrinal judgments for church practice.

The two churches reflected on are the Church of God, Pillar of the Truth Church, which is one of the increasing numbers of independent pentecostal churches of the Deep South, and the Rock of Life Church, which finds itself among the multiple urban, independent pentecostal churches of New England. Both churches are independent Pentecostal-type churches. Yet, doctrinal practices regarding women's roles and attire reveal in different ways the theological conflicts among Scripture, the Church and culture.

Situation at the Rock of Life Church

The Rock of Life Church (ROLC) was founded in the mid twentieth century as part of the classical pentecostal denomination, the "United Pentecostal Church (UPC)." Traditionally, the UPC maintained strict dress codes that prohibited women from wearing pants, using make-up, cutting their hair and the ordination of women preachers. From that time till now, the church has separated from the UPC denomination. Though the church has not changed its name, it is no longer a UPC church. ROLC currently remains charismatic and falls within the parameters of what I have defined as an independent pentecostal-type church. The current pastor is Pastor Ray Rivers, an African American male.

Rivers was a business executive in corporate America. Aside from his "on-the-job" training as a lay minister, Rivers had little formal theological training. Upon discerning the call of God on his life, Rivers left a corporate career to become full-time senior pastor. Under Pastor Rivers' leadership, the church has become increasingly ethnically diverse, comprised of African Americans, European Americans, Trinidadian Americans, Jamaican Americans, and Latin Americans, and remains an independent, pentecostal-type church. To the Rev. Rivers' credit, a church that was once affiliated with one of the most racist and segregated pentecostal bodies of the early twentieth century in the United States of America[5] is now very ethnically diverse. The church is vibrant and attracts many young people and many others across the age spectrum, including recovering drug addicts and alcoholics.

Currently, the church is not connected to the UPC. Consequently, it does not consciously adhere to doctrinal practices of its former affiliation. However, in practice, the church seems to struggle to define its doctrinal practice on issues of baptismal formula and the inclusion of women in ordained ministry. Traditionally, Pastor Rivers handles the tough questions simply by not publically confronting them as important for the new direction of the church.

ROLC has grown from a few members to approximately 5,000. The pastor possesses strong interpersonal skills and is attentive to people's day-to-day needs, such as food and housing. He is patient with people, and is a well-rounded, gifted leader. He has a strong work ethic. Pastor Rivers is the only pastor on staff at the church. After almost ten years and despite the demands of the growing church for more than one pastor, Pastor Rivers remains reluctant to share the authority of the church with an associate or assistant pastor. His workdays are long.

As the church's unilateral senior leadership, Pastor Rivers is quiet on controversial doctrine and practices. He usually avoids engaging controversial conversations concerning the ordination of women, "holy attire," baptismal formula, and *glossalalia* (speaking in tongues as initial evidence of the baptism of the Holy Spirit) – all of which have been important issues among pentecostal-type churches for more than a century.

Problem as Illustrated at the Rock of Life Church

I served at ROLC as an instructor in the Victorious Living Course Series. I taught a course (for people in the pews" called New Testament Survey. While in class one night, a student raised the issue of the ordination of women as pastors, apostles, evangelists, and bishops. At the time, I was unclear on the church's theological position on the issue. There is no written statement on the issue in the church's polity or in its Articles of Faith. And there is little public discussion on these issues.

The only female to preach on a Sunday morning while I attended the church was the pastor's wife. She only spoke to the women on mother's day. She is not an ordained minister. In fact, with the exception of the senior pastor, the church has not ordained anyone – male or female -- in the seven years of the pastor's tenure. The pastor does not discuss the ordination of aspiring ministers (men nor women), nor does he publicly acknowledge the ordination of ministers who were ordained prior to joining the ROLC. In this way, he distances the complex theological and ecclesiological issues that might emerge.

Pastor Rivers is careful not to allow theological and ecclesiological issues to challenge his leadership. Such discussions could possibly impede the numerical and perhaps what he would consider the spiritual growth of the church. However, since he does not address these critical issues, there is no clear, critical theological basis for the doctrinal practices of ordination. Therefore, when asked that evening in my class about the ordination of women, I responded from my own theological perspective, which supports the ordination of women. I realized that I did not know the doctrinal stance of the church, much less the theological arguments that support it.

After the class, I shared with the pastor all the questions raised, including the question on the ordination of women. In response, he insisted that, in the future, when such questions arise, I should say to students, "You should speak with Pastor Rivers about that." It seems that there is neither a clear theological formula nor a consistent set of criteria – written or verbal – for the church's doctrinal practice. As result, the congregation, although numerically strong with programs effective in church growth, seems unequipped in tools for wrestling with theological questions.

Views on Scripture at the Rock of Life Church

In his sermons, Pastor Rivers asserts that the Bible is the "inerrant" Word of God. He often suggests that the words on the page reflect the mind of God, and are to be adopted as the Word of God for today. Yet, I am often perplexed when I observe practices that suggest otherwise. For example, Rivers does not seem to believe that women should be silent in the church,[6] since his wife occasionally preaches there. He does not believe that "slaves"[7] should obey their masters. In fact, he often speaks on the equality of all people. One wonders if he is applying a revisionist interpretation of scripture unexplained. If so, the literalist language and fundamentalist claim on the inerrancy of scripture is misleading. The problem appears to emerge from the convergence of scriptural interpretation and culture in the teachings of the church.

The pastor's ideas and practices illustrate further the nature of the theological problem encountered in this convergence. Pastor Rivers does not believe that a divorced person with a living ex-spouse should remain unmarried as long as the first spouse is alive."[8] He officiates at weddings of individuals who have been previously married, and he appoints as deacons persons who have been divorced and remarried. It is, therefore, clear that Pastor Rivers' leadership does not reflect a belief that the Bible is the "inerrant" Word of God. Contrary to claims, moreover, practice suggests that there may be some other criteria, in addition to Scripture, at work in shaping theological judgments and doctrinal practices at ROLC. However, those criteria are not articulated.

Views on Experiences of the Holy Spirit at the Rock of Life Church

At ROLC, elements of pentecostal spirituality are important. Particularly, the church values experiences of the Holy Spirit, namely prophecy, speaking in tongues and the interpretation of tongues, dreams, and visions. Often, during the song service, someone would freely approach the pastor or pass a note to him to let him know that he or she has a word of prophecy from God to share with the congregation. If the pastor discerns the movement to be an authentic move of God fitting for the service, he would spontaneously insert this unexpected action into the order of service. He often explains that God is in charge of the service, and that he has to make room for the Holy Spirit. As the pastor permits, the individual inspired to prophesy would address the congregation.

The person upon whom the gift of prophesy has descended, would say, often in both the rhetoric of old English and contemporary Standard English, probably derived from reading the King James Version of the Bible: "Thus saith the

Lord... Truly saith the Lord." This rhetoric is familiar to me as it is reminiscent of my classical-pentecostal heritage. After the prophetic word has been spoken, the congregation would applaud in recognition of the voice of God in prophesy. As with many pentecostal-type churches, at the Rock of Life Church, prophecy is a regular activity during the song service.

Also, speaking in tongues is important at the Rock of Life Church as a gift of the Holy Spirit to aid the believer in prayer. Yet, similar to the so-called neo-pentecostal movements and unlike the classical pentecostal movements of its heritage, the church does not subscribe to beliefs of initial evidence. People are encouraged to speak in tongues as a spiritual exercise of communicating with God in a language that is beyond human comprehension. Thus, speaking in tongues is spiritual communication with God in a way that the human self cannot activate, except by the Holy Spirit. In short, experiences of the Holy Spirit are central to the spiritual life of the church. Speaking in tongues is welcomed as a possible means through which God will intervene in the communal worship experience to communicate a message to the worshipping community. Yet, speaking in tongues as a means of communicating a message to the congregation, accompanied by the interpretation of tongues, is seldom exercised in this congregation. Several people at ROLC who profess the baptism of the Spirit pray in tongues but others who profess Spirit-baptism have never spoken in tongues.

Views on Culture at the Rock of Life Church

To accommodate cultural diversity at ROLC in the planning of the church's annual calendar, the pastor avoids holding services for holidays and festivals that celebrate the African American heritage and contribution to the American society, namely "Martin Luther King Day" and "Black History Month." He does not specify which celebrations might be antithetical to the faith. His rationale is that in an ethnically diverse congregation it is wise to stay away from ethnic-specific celebrations. There might be a request to participate in an ethnic celebration that violates the church's religious stance. So, to avoid confusion later, no ethnic specific celebrations are permitted, namely the ones that highlight the African American experience and contribution to the development of American society. In recognition of cultural diversity, the church hosts an annual celebration called "A Taste of the Rock," a banquet-style event which includes national dishes from all the cultures represented in the congregation.

Culture does have prominence in other forms. Because there are several veterans in the church and families with loved ones who were casualties of war, the pastor designates the Sunday nearest Veterans Day as a time to honor the sacrifice and legacy of those who put their lives on the line for America. Usually, volunteers in military service at ROLC perform a ceremony. At times, Rev. Rivers, like many other pastors, devotes part of his sermon to honoring military personnel and providing special prayer for those at war in Iraq and Afghanistan.

Moreover, similar to preceding examples, the lack of a clearly defined role of culture in doctrinal practices suggests a lack of expressed appreciation for the role of African Americans in the struggle for justice in the United States. It seems, however, that Rivers is willing to provide room for civil, rather than ethnic, categories of culture, in order to minimize possible conflicts on ethnicity at ROLC. However, concerning African American heritage, it is extremely difficult to so neatly separate the ethnic cultural experience and contributions from the civil cultural experience and contributions. Hence, the role of culture requires critical review for the theological enterprise at ROLC. In a sense, these doctrinal practices may perpetuate racial oppression for African Americans and esteem the agenda of war higher than the histories of African American contribution to American society, not only in the church, but also among American citizens as they live in the world beyond the context of the church.

The pastor at ROLC presents what seems to be a theological contradiction. He, on the one hand, screens cultural celebrations to the point of excluding the observance of an important month for African Americans and the celebration of those who have helped to transform the plague of racism and bigotry in this country, such as Martin Luther King. In addition, African American History Month is an opportunity for the entire nation to focus on the lives and legacies of a population systematically minimized in or excluded from the formal history of the country. On the other hand, the pastor freely holds celebrations and tributes for occasions that have no clear connection to ethnic or race relations in America. So then, is it theologically acceptable for Rev. Rivers to acknowledge war-related celebrations in America, but theologically "unwise" to acknowledge the achievements of cultures abused by the injustice of the dominant culture?

It seems that the role of culture in theological judgments and doctrinal practice at ROLC is compromised by a distorted ethnic cultural critique. Therefore, as ROLC clearly illustrates, certain forms of culture are appropriate to church practice. Yet, the role of culture is ambiguous in making theological judgments for doctrinal practice.

The issue of cultural celebrations is important as it points to a deeper issue. The majority of the members of ROLC are citizens of the urban communities that surround the church. Most of whom are victims of marginalization related to their ethnicities, namely of African and Hispanic descent. African American History Month is a time to highlight and celebrate how God has blessed our country in the process of overcoming histories of injustice. It is, also, a time to advance the value of ethnic cultural kaleidoscope that makes up the global Christian community. Any intentional avoidance to celebrate ethnic diversity in this country by default lifts the dominant culture as the only one with true sacred worth. A church originally affiliated with UPC, though in many ways far removed from poisonous racism of its ancestry, has not come to the full integration of ethnic cultural integration as part of its Church practice.

Situation at the Church of God, Pillar of the Truth Church

The Church of God, Pillar of the Truth Church (COGPOTC), is 97%-99% African American. With several denominational and theological influences, the Church of God, Pillar of the Truth Church emerged from a local Church of God in Christ congregation as an independent church. Elder Leroy Williams planted this church in late twentieth century. Like many other pastors and aspiring pastors, he had a deep love for God and an intense search for truth. Aside from his home church's Bible studies, he attended small Bible studies with pastors from other denominations. Also, Williams testifies of personal religious experiences that guided his developing beliefs. Many of them collided with pre-understandings based on COGIC doctrinal practices. For example, the young pastor's teachings were influenced by the "in Jesus' name" baptismal formula of the Apostolic Pentecostal Movement, and the exclusion of women from the preaching ministry of the church. The Church of God, Pillar of the Truth Church is now a small, independent church of approximately 1,000 members, yet, because of its rich theological heritage of pentecostal-type traditions, this congregation, like most independent pentecostal churches, represents a conflation of doctrinal practices from various church traditions.

Problem Illustrated at the Church of God, Pillar of the Truth

Being influenced by some of the teachings of ministers from the Way of the Cross – an Apostolic Holiness denomination of African descent – and his own interpretation of the Bible, strictly from the King James Version,[9] the Elder Williams began teaching doctrines contrary to those of the Church of God in Christ: 1) the Trinitarian formula of baptism is inconsistent with biblical practice in the early Church; and 2) it is contrary to God's order for the church that women preach. Therefore, God would not contradict God's own "Word" and call a woman to preach; therefore, the church should not permit women to preach. Interestingly, COGIC, to this day does not ordain women to preach and does not allow them to vote on certain matters pertaining to the church. Yet, these stipulations were not enough for Elder Williams. For him, women should not preach at all. Williams left COGIC and started an independent church.

Views on Scripture at the Church of God, Pillar of the Truth

The Church of God, Pillar of the Truth Church regards Scripture an esteemed role in the development of church doctrine and practice. For more than thirty years, COGPOTC has maintained the two church doctrinal practices cited above as the unwavering doctrinal foundations of the church. These doctrines are thought to be responsible for the split from the Church of God in Christ. Any other doctrine is built around and in addition to these doctrines, but never contrary to them. These pillars are the single set of hermeneutical lenses for biblical interpretation in this church and the official hermeneutical lenses for interpreting experiences of the Holy Spirit. Even the gospel is attached to these pillars, such that the church determines one's acceptance of the gospel and quality of relationship with God based on acceptance of the church's doctrinal practices.

II Peter 1:20 (KJV) states, "Knowing this first, that no prophecy of the Scripture is of any private interpretation. For the prophecy came not in old time by the will of man: but holy men of God spake as they were moved by the Holy Ghost." Pastor Williams explains that this passage means that there is no private interpretation of any Scripture in the old or new testaments. Therefore, he, like many traditional pentecostal-holiness pastors, teaches that the Holy Spirit inspires his explanation of Scripture. He therefore believes that if anyone is inspired by the Holy Ghost, that person would have the same interpretation of Scripture.

Having never received formal theological training, Rev. Williams believes that he has access to divinely revealed universal truth. By universal truth, this congregation believes that the interpretation of Scripture that the pastor provides is the single explanation to which the "Church universal" should subscribe as authentic practice of God's will for all of humanity. The Rev. Williams represents pastors whose unilateral explanation of Scripture becomes the foundation of all doctrinal practice for the congregation.

Views on Experiences of the Holy Spirit at the Church of God, Pillar of the Truth

Experiences of the Holy Spirit are essential to faith at COGPOTC. The language used here – experiences of the Holy Spirit – refers to the revelatory moments whereby one claims to have heard the voice of God, whether through dreams, visions, or through the speaking of God through *glossalalia* (speaking in and interpreting tongues). For example, speaking in Tongues is central to the baptism of the Holy Spirit. Consistent with its C.O.G.I.C. heritage, speaking in tongues remains the initial evidence that an individual has received the baptism of the Spirit. In addition, the church values dreams, visions and personal revelations as essential to the experience of the Holy Spirit.

However, the spiritual experiences of the senior pastor take precedence over anyone else's experiences in the formation of doctrine or communal doctrinal practice. The Rev. Williams claims several experiences wherein the Holy Spirit showed him, spoke to him, or in some way, communicated directly with him. Like many pastors, the Rev. Williams seems to believe that there is no truth that challenges his own interpretation of what is right or wrong. This means that his own experience is God's revelation of universal truth. His interpretations of doctrinal truths are the lenses through which he seems to view not only truth for his own church but truth for the world. Such high claim of universal truth (per revealed to him) excludes any theological discourse with others. If one does not have the same revelation he has or if one is not willing to accept and practice the revelations he claims, he distances himself from their fellowship. Therefore, the parishioners look to the Rev. Williams for him to validate their experiences of the Holy Spirit. In other words, they would right-off their own insights and revelatory experiences if they do not seem consistent with those of the pastor. In short, if one offers a revelation contrary to that of the pastor, the reported revelation is not critically engaged for the possibility of dismissal or even reinterpretation of existing doctrinal practice. Rather, the parishioner's experience is often marginalized or even demonized thereby excluded as possible theological discussion pertaining to revising doctrinal practices.

The foregoing is illustrated by the following example: if a woman professes to have had an experience of the Holy Spirit wherein God called her to ordained ministry, the pastor does not validate her experience and denies her the opportunity to enter ordained ministry. Instead of acceptance, the woman's submissive character is called into question. Her own alleged experience that might testify to her call to the ministry is negated based on interpretations of Scripture used to formulate doctrine that excludes women from ordained ministry. The church does not give audience for theological challenge based on experiences with the Holy Spirit that seem to affirm women in ministry.

Another example of the problems between theological tenets of the church and church practices concerns the issue of women's "holy attire," or more specifically, the prohibition on wearing pants. Contemporary young women who desire to join the church find the prohibition of women-wearing-pants an oppressive teaching. When they challenge this doctrinal practice, the pastor encourages the young women to pray. In some cases, young women return (from prayer) professing that God showed them that wearing pants is permissible. Others return and confess that God showed them that they should not wear pants. In both cases, the women lay claim on experience with the Holy Spirit through which God spoke to them. However, only the spiritual experiences of women who come into compliance with the pastor's interpretation are validated. Therefore, at the Church of God, Pillar of the Truth Church, experiences of the Holy Spirit are valued highly as criteria for doctrine and doctrinal practices, but are intensely appraised by the discernment of the senior pastor.

Views on Culture at the Church of God, Pillar of the Truth

This book focuses on the theological problem exposed in doctrine regarding women's dress and women in ordained ministry. With reference to the prohibition on women wearing pants, the doctrinal practice is based on Deuteronomy 22:5: "The woman shall not wear that which pertaineth unto a man, neither shall a man put on a woman's garment: for all that do so are abomination unto the LORD thy God" (KJV). Based on this passage, the teaching is that the wearing of pants by women is an abomination to the Lord.[10] To reinforce the church's position on the issue, Pastor Williams posted a typewritten sign on the front door of the church, which announced: "Women wearing trousers and men wearing dresses are not permitted in the sanctuary." The pastor often adamantly declared that, even if women in the larger society wear pants, it is wrong, denying that culture has any divine role in matters pertaining to theological matters affecting church doctrinal practice.

On occasion, designated persons in the church dismiss female visitors who arrived at the church wearing pants. A few times, I personally observed female visitors wearing pants who managed to make it through the church doors. However, to reinforce this restriction, and accommodate women who might not know the rules, designated persons (usually ushers, deacons or ministers) kindly offer a dress or skirt to visitors.

To further enforce this doctrine, couples planning to be married must include a note in their wedding invitation that states, "Women wearing pants and men wearing skirts or dresses will not be admitted into the sanctuary." At times, family and friends of church members who travel from far distances to attend weddings and funerals are warned not to wear pants. There have been occasions when a woman wearing pants to a wedding or funeral has not been allowed in the sanctuary. At times, visiting women arrive for services or special events wearing pants, read the posted sign, and leave the premises without discussion.

There appears to be a contradiction in the implementation of this restriction at COGPOTC on two fronts:

1. The Church of God, Pillar of the Truth Church places a high value on academic achievement. They operate a K-12 primary school – Victorious Life Academy. During graduations and other academic ceremonies, the entire educational ministry board, faculty and graduating class wears academic regalia – including robes, hoods and caps.

2. Each week, during the main worship service and at all convocations and revivals, the ministers (men) wear clergy regalia – including long robes.

Some young people are now challenging the issue of dress restrictions, questioning the logic of academic robes shared by men and women, as well as the apparent contradiction in (male) ministers wearing long robes when women are forbidden to wear pants. As indicated here, church practices seem to contradict the communal interpretation of Deuteronomy 22:5. If, according to this interpretation of the text, men and women should not both wear pants or dresses or skirts, it is inconsistent with that interpretation for male preachers to wear robes ("…a woman's garment") in that the women are expected to wear only dresses or skirts.

Many problems emerge from this debate, but the main concern here is the role of culture within biblical interpretation in the formation of church doctrine and doctrinal practices. I recognize that the example of "holy attire" may not bear a critical analysis well due to the circular logic employed in the church practice. Nevertheless, this example helps to expose the hermeneutical and theological issues of interest. The COGPOTC is not trapped in this theological predicament alone. Many other pentecostal-type churches perpetuate similar theological quandaries in the formulation of their doctrinal practice. Some of them emphasize the issue of dress less but are closed minded to other cultural issues such as Hip Hop music or Rock styles of music as part of the worship.

Final Reflections

These examples reflect deep theological problems in the convergence of Scripture, experiences of the Holy Spirit, and culture, i.e., the trilateral, in doctrinal practices among many independent pentecostal churches of the African Diaspora. The two churches described are in some ways different and in other ways quite similar. The thread of commonality connecting the two churches is that they are independent pentecostal-type churches with pastors who make unilateral theological judgments for church doctrinal practices. Both pastors are gifted leaders. They value highly the roles of Scripture, experiences of the Holy Spirit and of culture in shaping doctrinal practice. Yet, the pastoral leadership of these cases represents a wider constituency of pentecostal-type churches that delivers doctrinal practices that are not reflective of a critical theological analysis of Scripture, experiences of the Holy Spirit and culture.

Incidentally, both churches place a high value on Scripture, experiences of the Holy Spirit and culture as important in making theological judgments for church doctrinal practices. Yet, there is inconsistency in how these three criteria are treated in making those judgments. The inconsistency creates conflicting claims between certain interpretations of Scripture, activity of the Holy Spirit, and perceptions of culture. As illustrated above, church polity and theological rationales for doctrinal practices are oppressive to the community, mainly women. An impasse emerges between authoritative claims on the gifts or revelations of the Spirit and interpretations of Scripture regarding not only women's ordination, but also lay participation in worship and church ministries.

This impasse illustrates only one of the paradigmatic problems exposed in the relationship between ecclesiology and church practices among independent pentecostal-type churches.

Notes

1. See numbers at Todd M. Johnson, "Three Waves of Christian Renewal: A 100-Year Snapshot," *International Bulletin of Missionary Research,* (Vol. 30, No 2, April 2006), 76.

2. Ibid., 75, 76.

3. Douglas Jacobsen, *Thinking in the Spirit: Theologies of the Early Pentecostal Movement* (Bloomington, IN: Indiana University Press, 2003), 12

4. Later, I explain that the implications of the gospel for Christian theology are both the affirmation of a variety of cultural practices (even changing cultural practices) and the critique of them to avoid contaminating the message of the gospel.

5. Roswith I. H. Gerloff. *A Plea for British Black Theologies: The Black Church Movement in Britain in its Transatlantic Cultural and Theological Interaction* (New York: Peter Lang, 1992), see chapter 3.

6. I Corinthians 14: 34-35.

7. Titus 2:9.

8. Mark 10:11-12.

9. Pastor Leroy Williams is committed to the King James Version of the Bible and continues to use it as the official Bible in his church. He discourages his congregation from interpretations suggested by other translations. He understands other translations to be the product of the human search for self-righteousness, appeasing themselves with alternative routes to truth.

10. The Church of God, Pillar of the Truth, "Affirmation of Faith" (1999), 1-2.

Chapter 3
Culture: Theological Criterion or Theological Enemy?

The problems highlighted in these illustrations raise an immediate question: What relationship among interpretations of Scripture, experiences of the Holy Spirit, and perceptions of culture, would help reshape oppressive doctrinal practices?

The role of culture presents a challenge in making theological judgments for doctrinal practices. In both congregations, the Rock of Life Church and the Church of God, Pillar of the Truth Church, the role of culture seems important. However, the manner in which culture is applied in theological discourse and church doctrine is often confusing. On the one hand, both churches seem to be deeply culturally sensitive in, for example, their music and worship expressions. On the other hand, they seem to *evade* culture as a theological tenet in doctrinal matters with Scripture and the Holy Spirit. This issue has had profound consequences. For example, the inability of church leaders to critically engage culture in making theological judgments for doctrinal practice has resulted in practices that are oppressive, particularly to women.

Oppression is antithetical to the liberating mission of Jesus. This mission is stated in Luke 4:18-19: "The Spirit of the Lord is upon me, because he has anointed me to preach the gospel to the poor; he has sent me to heal the brokenhearted, to preach deliverance to the captives and recovery of sight to the blind, to set at liberty them that are bruised, to preach the acceptable year of the Lord" (NSRV). Summing up the mission of Jesus, Paul asserts, "Worthy is the saying and approved for all acceptance, that Christ Jesus came into the world to deliver sinners, of which I am the chief" (I Tim 1:15, an original translation).

In his commentary of this passage, Bongani A. Mazibuko states:

> Jesus came to save all sinners; consequently, if his ministry is the model of ours then the aim of our ministry must be to enable people to discover for themselves that the statement that Christ Jesus came into the world to save all sinners is completely reliable and should be universally accepted. To sin is something more serious than to offend against some principle or standard; to sin is to destroy our relationship to ourselves; to other people; to the natural world and to God.[1]

Building on Mazibuko's commentary of I Tim 1:15, Nico Botha explains that "Sin is not only personal, individual sin, but takes on social and structural forms. To be saved or liberated from sin is consequently not only an issue of being saved or liberated from some hidden, individual sin, but for the oppressed it may mean the *liberation from suffering,* and for the oppressors the *liberation from sin.*"[2] Therefore, engaging culture as a theological criterion for producing doctrinal practices, which do not perpetuate oppression for anyone,[3] is consistent with the mission of the gospel of Christ. Any proposed theological process for building doctrine for a church of the Lord Jesus Christ must be vigilantly achieved through re-imaging the process for ascertaining theology for church communities that is faithful to the mission of Jesus, a mission stated in the gospels and echoed in Paul's writings.

How can the church understand Scripture through the lens of culture(s) and in light of religious experiences to establish doctrine consistent with the liberating nature of the gospel? The issue of "holy attire" has split many pentecostal-type congregations. The issue of women wearing pants is an old debate among pentecostal churches. One would imagine that over time, this issue would dissolve with simple cultural logic. However, this issue is yet the subject of intense debate within pentecostal-type churches.

I have chosen to address this somewhat superficial discussion because it is a real, concrete situation deserving of theological scrutiny. This discussion appropriately and relevantly illustrates the deeper problem of culture and the way in which it informs biblical hermeneutics as revealed in doctrinal practices. Therefore, while the discussion of "holy attire" may seem superficial, its superficiality exposes the dire need to scrutinize the deeper theological issue at hand. This deeper theological problem manifests itself in doctrinal practices which are particularly oppressive to women. Many women in these two churches comply with the oppressive teachings, having accepted them as the "Word of God."

The issue of "holy attire" emerged as paramount at several churches and at the Church of God, Pillar of the Truth. This issue is rooted in the pentecostal church tradition, since the early twentieth-century.

However, the problem of "holy attire" is rooted, not in sound interpretations of Scripture (i.e., Deut. 22:5), but within America's culturally-dominant, normative standards of attire in the early twentieth century. So then, even in the earliest period of American pentecostalism (whether intentionally or unintentionally), culture played a role in biblical interpretations. During that period, for the most part, men wore pants or trousers and women wore dresses or skirts. However, this division in traditional male and female attire was influenced by a shift in cultural norms during the mid- to late twentieth century. This shift challenged interpretations of Scripture previously applied to church doctrinal practices that prohibited women in pentecostal churches from wearing trousers because doing so is "an abomination" to God.[4] In addition, some independent pentecostal churches have elevated the issue of "holy attire" to the centrality of the pentecostal experience, as illustrated at the Church of God, Pillar of the Truth Church (described in Chapter 1).

This sustained topic (around the world) of "holy attire" speaks to the critique of culture derived from scriptural interpretations in the early days of the pentecostal movement. Efforts among pentecostal-type churches to maintain those readings speak to the need for such churches to re-interpret Scripture in light of altered cultural norms and subsequently reshape church practices.

Some independent pentecostal churches struggle with the relationship among interpretations of Scripture, experiences of the Holy Spirit and perceptions of culture in the development of doctrinal practices. It is ironic, as Allan Anderson aptly states, "[T]he expansion of the pentecostal 'full gospel' in the twentieth century all over the world can be attributed, at least partially, to cultural factors."[5] Yet, since the emergence of the global movement early last century, there has been increased debate over the interrelationship of Scripture, the Spirit, and culture. The struggle over "culture" in theological discourse has resulted in the splintering of many independent pentecostal churches.

Pentecostal-type Christians place primary importance on Scripture as the normative theological authority. Although similar claims are made by other American Protestant denominations and congregations, pentecostal-type churches provide a distinctive model for understanding Scripture as a unique theological norm. In other words, *sola scriptura* looks very different in the hands of a pentecostal-type preacher than it does in the hands of a Lutheran preacher.

The pentecostal preacher clings to Scripture as God's Word. He or she expects a continued charismatic experience of the gifts of the Sprit, gifts such as speaking in tongues, prophesying, and healings as manifestation of God and proof that God's Word is alive and in operation within the church. Additionally, the pentecostal preacher expects the Holy Spirit to both illumine scripture for understanding and application in the life of the church and thereby the everyday lives of the believers. Similarly to the pentecostal preacher, the Lutheran preacher expects the Holy Spirit to illumine the biblical text for understanding and application. However, the Lutheran preacher, unlike the pentecostal preacher, does not expect a continued charismatic experience as proof that God's Word is alive and in operation in the church. The goal is to determine the role of the Holy Spirit and culture within scripture as guide in making coherent and consistent theological judgments for the transformation of such practices in a reshaped ecclesiology. Thus, for the pentecostal-type churches any potentially transformative analysis of ecclesiology must, of necessity, involve an examination of the Bible and the discipline of biblical interpretation as integral role to aid in Biblical interpretation and Scriptural application.

Gospel and Culture

Throughout history of Christianity, church leaders and theologians have noted the intricate relationship between the gospel and culture in Scripture. Yet, scholars and church leaders have varying interpretations of how these two concepts interrelate.

In his classic *Christ and Culture,* H. Richard Niebuhr presents a taxonomy of five "zones" to aid in understanding this relationship. The first is "Christ against culture." In this zone, Christ is not adaptable to culture; rather, Christ is contrary to culture. Consequently, one way Christians respond to culture is to withdraw from society.[6]

The second zone is "Christ of culture." This zone emphasizes a viable relationship between Christ and culture. Jesus fully embodies the greatest human aspirations while he is also the ultimate hero of human culture, and represents the very best human product of culture. Therefore, there is a close relationship between loyalty to Christ and the best offering of a particular culture.[7]

The third zone is "Christ above culture." This zone affirms the synthesis between Christ and culture. Christ is Master of this world and the other. The two worlds are not perceived as separate. Christ bridges the material world and the *meta*-physical world in his complex human/divine nature. Christ is from above but enters the physical world through culture. Christ comes with gifts that human aspiration has not envisioned and which human effort cannot attain. The only way for human beings to attain knowledge of such gifts is through the teachings and example of Christ, i.e., the gospel. Christ, therefore, affirms and analyzes culture.[8]

The fourth zone is "Christ and culture in paradox." In this zone, there is less continuity between culture and Christianity. Rather, the paradox accentuates the ongoing dissonance between Christ and human culture. Niebuhr identifies proponents of this zone as dualists as they recognize the duality of law and grace, wrath and mercy, revelation and reason, and time and eternity. Through divine providence, God exposes metaphysically God's own will.[9]

The fifth zone is "Christ, the transformer of culture." This zone offers an optimistic vision of the relationship between Christ and culture. Christ represents and initiates the hope of cultural renewal. As transformer, Christ's incarnation is an embrace of culture for the goal of transforming culture from self-centeredness to Christ-centeredness.[10]

Since the gospel is the message of Christ, Niebuhr's taxonomy is relevant to this current treatment of the gospel and culture. My position on the relationship between gospel and culture exists on a continuum and functions as interplay among three zones in the taxonomy, namely zones two, four and five. Thomas H. Groome and other theologians use the term *inculturation*. Their use of *inculturation* acknowledges the helpful role of culture(s) in the incarnation of Jesus and the expansion of the early church.[11] Niebuhr does not offer a category for Christ "with" culture, Christ "adapted to" culture, or Christ "translated in" culture. The aim here is to clarify a relationship of Christ that is out of culture, other than culture, and the hope of culture, yet simultaneously adaptable to culture.

The gospel emerged from the cultural history of the Jewish people. At the time of Jesus, in the Greco-Roman world, Jewish culture was heavily influenced by Hellenism. A basic example of this influence is language. First-century Jews spoke *koine* (common language of the people) Greek and Hebrew. Amidst this culturally rich society, Jesus introduced a message to address the needs of Jewish people, as well as the needs of people from other cultural heritages. The gospel's ability to speak to the needs of culturally diverse populations is a positive indication of the unique nature of the message of Jesus.

Michael Goheen argues that the gospel stands in a dialogical relationship with any ethnic culture it encounters. It does not simply shout an imperialistic "no" to culture and offer a replacement or an alternative. Rather, the gospel affirms and embraces the "good" in all cultural environments.[12] Furthermore, the gospel can appropriate various cultural models without entirely assimilating into them. Lamin Sanneh calls this unique character the continuing "translatability of the gospel."[13] The gospel is translatable, in that it can affirm the stories, signs, and symbols of the vernacular. At the same time, the gospel is resistant to cultural assimilation, i.e., in that it affirms and reviews the vernacular. The gospel gives new meaning to old expressions of culture, according to its own interior norms.

Defining the Gospel in Light of Culture

The Synoptic Gospels express the major themes of the *kerygma*: the preaching of the gospel is "good news," not only to the unloved, alienated, and oppressed, but also to the loved, included, and liberated. It is God's expressed love for all humanity and God's revealed desire for the liberation of the oppressed – regardless of the basis for that oppression: ethnic, gender, spiritual, physical, or psychological. Paul's writings reveal his struggle with his own Jewish identity, an ethnicity characteristically oppressive to women. Yet, he makes frequent references to the "liberating Spirit,"[14] and the liberated life in Christ.[15] Paul suggests that the Holy Spirit initiates a new reality in Christ that is inclusive of "Jew and Gentile, male and female, slave and free."[16] Paul's own understanding of the power of the gospel is one of liberation. He struggles, however, to appropriate the fullness of that liberating power, primarily in his teachings on women's participation in the leadership of the church.[17]

This constant battle between the nature of the gospel and cultural predilections inhibits Paul's application of the liberating gospel to the oppressive patriarchal control of his Jewish upbringing. Perhaps, it is Paul's internal struggle that contributes to the apparent contradictions in his teachings, contradictions between the liberating Spirit of the gospel and his deeply-rooted chauvinism. I propose that these inconsistencies in Paul's work reveal his own internal process of liberating himself from the oppressive mindset of his Jewish upbringing.

Paul's Struggle

Paul's theological struggle in fully appropriating his newly discovered librating gospel to doctrinal matters may be evident in this confession in Phil. 3:7-12:
7. Yet, whatever gains I had, these I have come to regard as loss because of Christ. 8. More than that, I regard everything as loss because of the surpassing value of knowing Christ Jesus, my Lord. For his sake, I have suffered the loss of all things, and I regard them as rubbish, in order that I may gain Christ 9. And be found in him, not having righteousness of my own that comes from the law, but

one that comes through faith in Christ, the righteousness of God based on faith. 10. I want to know Christ....12. Not that I have already obtained him or have already reached the goal; but I press on to it, because Christ Jesus has made me his own. 13. Beloved, I do not consider that I have made it; but this one thing I do: forgetting what lies behind and straining forward to what lies ahead, 14.I press toward the goal for the prize of the heavenly call of God in Christ Jesus.

In verses 7 and 8, Paul references his firm subscription to Jewish theology and strict adherence to Jewish doctrine and practice prior to his conversion. He admits that his theological perspectives and ecclesiastical position as a Jew had placed him in a position of prominence among Jews.[18] His Jewish position of prominence is meaningful to him and his fellow Jewish brothers and sisters. Yet, because of his new discovery of Christ, he renounces a view that projects upon the gentiles both his theological subscription and ecclesiastical position esteemed as important within the religion of the Jews. In essence, Paul is reminiscing about having attained prominence as a Jewish leader, making judgments on appropriate and inappropriate Jewish practices amidst the Greco-Roman world. However, he admits that as a Christian minister, he has been successful in some areas, but is struggling in others, to grasp fully what it means to be "in Christ,"[19] or to adequately teach what it means for the church to embody the life and message of Christ.

Martin defines the language of "in Christ" as Paul's earnest desire to be ready for the return of Christ.[20] Martin interprets the language of "in Christ" in light of the eschatological language of "resurrection" in verses 10 and 11: "I want to know... the sharing of his (Christ's) sufferings by becoming like him in death; if somehow, I may attain the resurrection from the dead." In the above citation of the larger passage, I omitted these verses in order to draw attention to the broader theological dynamics within the text. It is not beyond this passage to conclude that "in Christ" means that Paul is striving for a better theological practice of the fullness of the gospel. Paul explains that although he has renounced his former theological commitments and now embraces the theology and community of Christ, he is yet wrestling with fully implementing the theology of the gospel. He indicates a struggle to separate himself from the practice of the "righteousness... that comes from the law."[21]

I agree with Hooker that this statement is not entirely eschatological, as some commentators seem to argue.[22] Some rudiments of Jewish theology find their way into Paul's theology. When he says, "righteousness...that comes from the law..." Paul may be struggling to break away from the former theologies of the Jewish faith, because he realizes that those ideas are antithetical to what it means to be "in Christ." He acknowledges the tension between his former commitments and his new call to be fully "in Christ." However, he also indicates his need to pull away from the influence of former pursuits to achieve this new calling from God to be "in Christ." He desires to incorporate these new theological concepts into the liberating Spirit of the gospel – a gospel devoid of oppression and exclusion on the basis of ethnicity, social position and gender.[23]

Continued Revelation

Paul admits his own struggle when he says, "Beloved, I do not consider that I have made it; but this one thing I do: forgetting what lies behind and straining forward to what lies ahead." Clearly, Paul is admitting his own humanity. In his humanity is the limitation of ability to appropriate fully the relationship of his faith in Christ to all areas needed in the church. In other words, in the above passage, I interpret Paul to be saying that the walk with Christ is of what I call *continued revelation*. *Continued revelation* means that Paul's theology is far from static and more of a "work-in-progress."[24] Understandably, if his theology is a work in progress, so are his teachings pertaining to applying the liberating gospel to ecclesiological and ecclesiastical matters. Perhaps, part of the "work in progress" is revealed in the lingering need in his writings to appropriate more clearly the gospel's liberating nature in affirming women's ministry in the church. Paul acknowledges the liberating nature of the gospel, mentioning his understanding of the Spirit that equalizes all believers in the eyes of God (I Cor. 12:13; Gal. 3:28; Col. 3:11).

In I Tim. 2:12 and I Cor. 14:34, Paul does not seem to leverage women's voices in the church to those of men. At the same time, Paul seems to understand the liberating nature of the gospel as he projects that liberation on cultural factions between Jews and Gentiles in regards to circumcision and non-circumcision. I contend, however, that Paul's writings, a) in Phil. 3:7-12: 7 reveal in Paul's own words his struggle to achieve all of the depth of theology revealed "in Christ." By doing so, Paul sets a precedent within the biblical church for what I call *continued revelation,* and b) in Gal 3:28 and Col 3:11, provide a platform for the contemporary Church to continue to extend the gospel's liberating nature as he did but to those areas in which he only was able to foretaste but was not able to fully address —particularly, the ordination of women in ministry and other matters.

Culture within Scripture

Paul's writings represent the work of a practical theologian sensitive to the adjudication of religious practices, such as circumcision, in light of the gospel. One scholar who would contend otherwise is Brad Ronnell Braxton. In his work, Braxton agrees with me that the gospel engages culture, and that it is antithetical to the nature of the gospel to exclude women from proclaiming its message.

Braxton uses Galatians as the primary text for his exegesis of the liberating gospel. In *No Longer Slaves: Galatians and African American Experience,* Braxton eloquently echoes Paul's polemic against slavery to the Galatians' oppressors as applicable polemic against ideological slavery that holds some African Americans in bondage.[25] Yet, in "The Role of Ethnicity," Braxton underestimates Paul's adjudication of culture in light of the gospel in Paul's newfound reality in Christ.

In this article, Braxton argues that in I Cor. 7:17-24, "Paul underestimated the role of ethnicity in configuring social existence."[26] He goes on to argue that Paul is so focused on constructing a "Christian" identity beyond the contemporary confines of ethnic identity, which he fails to affirm important cultural allegiances for both Jews and Gentiles. In addition, Braxton argues that in other writings (e.g., Rom 3:1-4; 9:1-11:36; Gal 2:15; I Thess 1:9), Paul is incapable of extricating from the discourse his own ethnically-conditioned assumptions and biases. Yet, he expects his readers to hold their own cultural assumptions and ethnic identities in abeyance or to eradicate them. It is a tactic Braxton labels "naïve."[27]

In contrast, Paul is not advocating a generic Christian identity. He is actively confronting ethnic tensions within his congregations, suggesting that they may find unity through their diversity. He is not demanding that congregants divest themselves of cultural identity. "Liberty in Christ" allows them to retain their ethnic personhood (Gal 2:4). By resisting the imposition of Jewish religious practices on non-Jewish believers (I Cor 7), Paul is, in fact, protecting the social location of every believer. This argument is supported by Paul's statement in I Cor 7:18-19:

> Was anyone called being circumcised? Let that person not become uncircumcised. Has any been called in uncircumcision? Let that one not be circumcised. Circumcision is nothing, and uncircumcision is nothing; but keeping the commandments of God."[28]

Although I will return to questions on circumcision later, it is significant now to note that, in I Corinthians 7:19, Paul refers to circumcision and uncircumcision as "nothing." In doing so, he is not devaluing either cultural practice. Rather, he is affirming them by including both as equal partners in the newfound faith in Jesus. Moreover, when Paul uses "nothing," he means that cultural commitment does not inhibit Christian identity. Contrary to Braxton, Paul affirms, rather than diminishes, cultural commitment.

This is not to say that the gospel's affirmation of culture is unqualified. It can be reasonably argued that the New Testament — particularly Acts 2, 10, 12, 15 and the Pauline corpus — projects an affirmative trajectory of theological intimacy between a liberating gospel and culture. While there is obvious inconsistency in theological application, particularly in Paul's writings, Paul and others have a theological vision of cultural affirmation. Perhaps, this theological vision provides a precedent for ongoing interaction between *kerygma* and culture, as the gospel continues to encounter new cultural contexts beyond Scripture. Mainline churches and their scholars have not adequately assessed this interplay between culture and message. Yet, independent pentecostal churches must take this interplay seriously as a more critical theological process towards reshaping doctrinal practices.

Despite the skepticism of some New Testament scholars, I want to focus attention on the importance of culture within Scripture, particularly in Paul's writings. My intent is to extract certain norms as guides to understanding the role of culture in the interpretation of Scripture for the twenty-first century. Scripture was indeed born out of a cultural context, both the ethnic-culture of the Jewish people and the broader cultural context of the Greco-Roman world. As the gospel expanded beyond Jews to other ethnic cultures, the gospel adapted to those groups, bringing good news of love and liberation to their respective situations. In bringing good news to these ethnic groups, Paul is one of the first to observe that the gospel affirmed the vernacular cultures of non-Jews with non-Jewish practices.[29] Consequently, if the twenty-first century church is to take Scripture seriously in reshaping its Christian identity -- i.e., in producing theological judgments for church doctrine and practices -- it is important to engage critically the positive vision of culture.

Pentecost

From the birth of the Church at Pentecost in Acts 2, the Spirit used cultural dynamics as a partner to bring about the *missio Dei* in and among all people, extending the family of God beyond the limits of the Hebrew people. Luke, the author of Acts, defends God's activity in the world, as new believers from various cultures encounter God. New Testament scholar Luke Timothy Johnson calls this God-human encounter theodicy "in the broadest sense."[30] That is to say, the writer intended to help believers visualize the encounter between God and human beings so that, regardless of their ethnic identity, they could identify with the story of God.

Non-Jews were not asked to become Jewish, or to change their cultural attire in order to be accepted into the family of God. Rather, their faith in Jesus Christ was sufficient. Non-Jews are welcome into full membership of the family of God.[31] They are not required to proselytize according to Jewish standards. Their acceptance has profound theological implications regarding cultural affirmation. Thus, "the salvation of the Gentiles" means that they are both saved as individuals, and they have become part of the family of God with the believing Jews as brothers and sisters, without having to adopt Jewish cultural customs.[32]

According to the account of Pentecost in Acts 2, "When the multitude came together... every person heard them (the ones who were baptized in the Holy Spirit) speak in one's own language."[33] Few New Testament scholars have noted that the unique activity of the Holy Spirit in Acts 2 affirms the presence of a variety of indigenous cultures. It appears, however, that no one who witnessed the outpouring of the Spirit at Pentecost was accustomed to religious experiences different from their own, as expressed in diverse cultures. This point we can surmise from two important questions in the text: "Look! Are not all of these which speak, Galileans? Nevertheless, how do we hear everyone in our own language, wherein we were born?"[34]

From Acts 2:1-13, one may infer that the initial uniqueness concerning the birth of the Church is the bridging of culture with the experience of Spirit baptism. Certainly, the Holy Spirit works miracles among people and affirms "everyone" in his or her birth language, so that they may see that there is no exclusively sacred culture in Christianity when it comes to "magnifying God."[35] This means that "peculiar people" are made peculiar, not by creating subcultural expressions to draw attention to themselves. Rather, they are peculiar people by the miracle of a gospel that transforms them such that they are "in the world, but not of it." "In the world, but not of it," means that they remain ethnically part of their own culture. No one could truly stand outside her or his own culture. However, new meaning and value can be ascribed to cultural symbols, signs and patterns. It is the miracle of being part *in* the world culturally, yet not *of* the world, because culture is examined through theological lens.

Sanneh asserts that the many tongues of Pentecost affirmed God's acceptance of all cultures within the scheme of salvation, reinforcing the position that Jews and Gentiles were equal before God.[36] In addition, the activity that signified the birth of the Church communicated that Christianity is adaptable to culture while Christianity also critiques culture. It becomes clear by the end of Acts 2, that cultural divides are not approved by the move of the Spirit and the birth of the Church. Rather, a certain transcendent character of the gospel empowers diverse cultures to maintain uniqueness, while coexisting with other cultures. In short, the Holy Spirit enables Christianity to adapt to culture. The Holy Spirit also welcomes culture into the Christian theological enterprise. These two characteristics of the Holy Spirit might be the resolution to theological tensions surrounding the role of culture in the theological enterprise.

First Jerusalem Council

The ability of the gospel to adapt to a variety of cultures was an objectionable concept to the believers from a Jewish background. This resulted in theological tensions that caused internal factions among Jewish Christians throughout the New Testament.[37] Glass notes that while the New Testament is grounded in the Jewish religion, Jews come from a multicultural background. Jewish boys were circumcised on the eighth day after birth. This practice was culturally essential for Jewish boys, and has been since the days of Abraham (Gen 17:9-14). However, the New Testament was written in *Koine* Greek.

Language is an essential element of culture. Therefore, by virtue of language the New Testament adapts to elements of ordinary life within the Greco-Roman culture. Jewish and Greek cultures came together in the New Testament. There were, of course, many points of convergence between them, but there were also notable clashes. One main clash concerned circumcision.[38] Greeks did not practice circumcision. When Jews became part of the Jesus movement, they maintained many of their Jewish practices as part of church doctrine. When Greeks joined the Jesus movement, however, the question became, which Jewish practices are required to become part of the Jesus movement?

Between Acts 2 and Acts 15, contentions arose among Jewish church leaders concerning the inclusion of Greeks without the requirement of circumcision. The gospel was progressive in such a way that those human subjects who pioneered its propagation were not theologically prepared. It was concern for the role of culture in doctrinal practices that initiated the need for the first council at

Jerusalem. The result of the first council was that circumcision was not a required doctrinal practice for Gentiles. It is important to note that the results were not that one should not be circumcised. Rather, the understanding is that the Hebrew cultural practice of circumcision would not be imposed upon those who do not subscribe to such a practice. This means that the gospel is adaptable to certain cultural practices.

Timothy Circumcised, Titus Uncircumcised: Culture as Theological Bedfellow

In Paul's congregations, culture was only legitimized according to its ability to serve as a vehicle for the gospel. When culture becomes a stumbling block to the perpetuation of the gospel of love and liberation, it ceases to be affirmed. This notion of legitimization is illumined by the example of male circumcision, a Jewish practice since the time of Abraham. Since post-exilic times, Jewish heritage was determined through one's maternal lineage. Jumping forward, it is important to note that Timotheus had a Jewish mother and a Greek father. Therefore, by post-exilic standards, he was Jewish. As a Jew, he was required to be circumcised. However, as a young man, he had not been circumcised. When Paul adopts Timotheus as a son in ministry, Paul instructs him to comply with the cultural practice of circumcision.[39] Still, Paul's focus is the perpetuation of the gospel. He writes in more than one instance that circumcision is not a requirement for salvation. Yet, he instructs Timotheus to be circumcised as he is called to preach the gospel primarily to Jews. His failure to adapt to that particular cultural practice would have been a stumbling block to Timotheus' ministry.

Paul, however, does not compel Titus to be circumcised, as Titus is a Gentile believer.[40] Titus is granted full access to the center of the faith community. Titus, like Timotheus, is one of Paul's protégés. Timotheus is compelled to sustain his cultural heritage for the sake of perpetuating the gospel. Paul seems to be saying that culture should not become a stumbling block to the spread of the gospel. In *A Commentary on St. Paul's Epistle to the Galatians*, Luther, Friedrich, Tischer and Schmucker argue that Paul's reason for not requiring Titus to be circumcised hinges upon a theological rationale asserted by the Judaizers. This rationale requires that non-Jews be circumcised or, in essence, subscribe to Jewish cultural practices in order to be acceptable to God. Paul resists the notion of a cultural prerequisite or validation.

The rationale for requiring Gentile Christians to be circumcised was that it is a necessary act to access the faith. While Paul did not condemn circumcision as an unprofitable practice for Jews, he argued that circumcision should not be practiced as a requirement of the gospel. Paul's Christian theology unleashes ties between the righteousness of God and cultural commitments. He understands that the inclusion of non-Jews requires the inclusion of non-Jewish cultures. To unleash the ties between one culture and righteousness is to free other cultures to join the household of God. Moreover, Paul rules that the compulsion to circumcise people as part of what it means for gentiles to become part of the family of

God in an insult to the gospel, and brings people's consciences into severe bondage.[41] Paul insists that Titus need not be circumcised. Having Titus circumcised would validate the Judaizers' argument that Christians must be circumcised. It would confuse Titus' targeted mission field of Gentiles and become a stumbling block to the propagation of the gospel.

Scholars have written much about the efforts to reconcile Gal 2:3 with Acts 16:3 (the case of Timothy's circumcision and Titus' uncircumcision). In their exegesis of Galatians, historical figures such as Luther, Friedrich, Tischer and Schmucker suggest (though not always with liberating arguments) that God's activity in Jesus Christ is denied in "affiance of requirement of circumcision."[42] They mean that when one adheres to the practice of circumcision, one denies God's activity in Jesus Christ. Therefore, the avoidance of circumcision is the new law for Christians as adherence to circumcision was the Jewish law of the Hebrew Bible. However, this explanation does not consider the Acts 16 account of Paul instructing Timothy to be circumcised.

Hans Dieter Betz reconciles Gal 2:3 with Acts 16:3 in his assertion that Paul is not resisting Jewish pressure in Gal 2:3, while he yields to it in Acts 16:3.[43] Rather, Titus is a Gentile, and Timothy is a Jew. Paul is not interested in denying Jewish rites, even for Christian Jews, nor is he interested in imposing Jewish rites upon non-Jews to validate their faith in Jesus Christ.[44] Most recently, in *Law in Paul's Thought,* Hans Hubner focuses on the relationship of law and gospel revealed in the text. He contends that Titus is not compelled to be circumcised as an implication of freedom from Jewish law as a whole.[45] Hubner understands Jewish law as bondage that intercepts the liberation found in the gospel. Therefore, for Hubner, the focus on avoiding circumcision is not to validate God's activity in Jesus as Luther, et al, suggest. Rather, the focus in Gal 2:3 is to accentuate freedom from Jewish law that the gospel makes possible. Yet, Hubner does not define liberation in the gospel in culturally affirming categories.

Moreover, I hasten to add that most scholars fail to draw out the important cultural affirmation in Paul's argument against circumcising Gentiles. Betz comes very close in his analysis of Gal 2:3 (as stated above). Betz asserts that in both Acts and Galatians Paul does not minimize the Jewish cultural practice of circumcision. Paul, rather, seeks to draw attention to "the liberty we have in Jesus Christ," which is Paul's reference to the gospel (Gal 2:4). The liberating character of the gospel affirms a variety of cultural expressions and practices as part of the continued story of God. When one accepts the gospel, one also accepts that the cultural milieu within which the gospel was born (i.e., Jewish culture) are not imposed alongside the gospel when it encounters another ethnic cultural context. Therefore, Christianity looks different, depending on the cultural traditions of the contexts within which it finds itself.

The liberating nature of the gospel is not limited to freedom from certain requirements of law. In fact, circumcision is not condemned in Paul's writings, as Luther, et al, contend. By denying "affiance of requirement of circumcision," Paul is not refuting the importance of such a practice for persons born Jewish;

rather, he is demonstrating the extension of the gospel to include people with other cultural backgrounds as part of the family of God.

Paul refutes circumcision as a passcode to the faith. In this sense, Paul is affirming Jewish culture for the Jews and affirming Greek culture for the Greeks. So then, Galatians is not a polemic against the law, but may be interpreted as an affirmation of cultural conflict over the requirements of the gospel.

Furthermore, Paul teaches that the prophecy that Abraham would be the father of many nations (*ethnos*) implies the inclusion of diverse cultures in the family of God. Therefore, multiple forms of culture are acceptable to the gospel, safeguarded by faith in its essential message.

Continuance of a Gospel that Affirms Culture

Contemporary Christians must continue the message of love and liberation that is adaptable to a variety of cultures and limited only by the gospel's own internal norms. This means that the liberating nature of the gospel remains constant, while it is simultaneously being integrated into various cultures. When the cultural adaptability of the gospel is not fully embraced, the message cannot be fully appropriated as the message that God intends. The gospel, therefore, seeks to infiltrate all of human societies through the gospel's ability to adapt to the kaleidoscope of cultures without being desecrated in the process.

Sanneh asserts that culture has always been an essential tool in transporting the essence of Christianity – the message of the gospel – into non-Jewish regions and among non-Jewish people.[46] We must remember that the gospel has a global mission. This global mission is made possible only through the ability of the gospel to adapt to a plethora of cultural contexts. In concert with Goheen and Sanneh, in her *Plea for British Black Theologies*, Roswith Gerloff adds that, "God is a living reality able to enter the depths of human lives,"[47] which involves a kaleidoscope of cultures. Gerloff's treatment of "independent pentecostal-type churches" in Gerloff's and Abraham Akrong's article for the *Global Atlas* called "Independents" beckons for a closer look at Christianity's capacity for cross-cultural transmission or cross-cultural transplantation.[48] In light of the growing cities, 'urbanization,' 'super giants,' or 'world class cities' that are market places for the exchange of knowledge and information, and from among the slum-dwellers coupled with the socially marginalized at the outskirts of glamour and capital, there are new developments of potential and the creation of a large educated middle class. In particular, young people of the world's 3,300 large metropolises actively seek solutions for society's instability, cultural paradoxes, generational conflicts, environmental changes, economic down-turns, health hazards, violence, and wars. Gerloff sees the cultural affinity of the gospel relevant to these cultural realities.[49] I believe that the transmission of the Christian message, as evidenced in its earliest manifestation (Acts 2) and extended in the ministry and teachings of Paul, allows for both fruitful dialogue and the appropriation of cultural diversity among the global community of churches. Therefore, on the local church level, Scripture must be interpreted in dialogue with local culture in order for the parties involved to formulate relevant doctrine and doctrinal practices.

Holy Spirit as Guide in Cultural Affirmation within Pentecostal History

The African American pentecostal movement of the twentieth century was sensitive to the culture-affirming character of the gospel to provide justice and liberation for African Americans. Thomas Gilmore, a veteran of the Civil Rights Movement, credits the Holy Spirit for guidance in the stride towards liberation for African Americans. Gilmore reports, "I consider myself a little mystical; I think most of us who came through the movement would say, 'I'm going to do what the Spirit says do, because I can't really predict what's going to happen tomorrow.' To me, that is the Spirit I'd been introduced to when I was younger. That was the Spirit my grandmother talked about, the *Holy* Spirit that would make her shout."[50] In short, Gilmore believes that liberation for oppressed African Americans was made possible by the guidance and inspiration of the Holy Spirit. In particular, the African American pentecostal church also emphasized the role of the Holy Spirit in working through African Americans to bring scriptural, as well as cultural, political, and social liberation.

The African American Church affirmed culture on two fronts: 1) the struggle of African Americans to gain liberation during the Civil Rights era; and 2) cultural affirmation in expressed worship. Primarily, the African American story, the particular history of as slaves and, later, as oppressed people in America, are intricate parts of African American culture.

African American pentecostal churches were supportive in the struggle for liberation in the Civil Rights era. During the Civil Rights Movement, the Black Church looked to the revealed experience of the Holy Spirit to expose the liberating promises of the gospel. This experience is described in Scripture: "The Spirit of the Lord is upon me, because he has anointed me to preach the gospel to the poor; he has sent me to heal the brokenhearted, to preach deliverance to the captives, and recovery of sight to the blind, to set at liberty them that are oppressed, to preach the acceptable year of the Lord."[51]

David James Randolph comments that in 1969, the centrality of biblical preaching kept the souls of African Americans alive, nourishing their spirits and providing a means to express publicly the collective struggle, and directing African Americans toward liberation.[52] The expressed inspiration through preaching that gave African Americans renewed hope was affirmed by the experience of the Holy Spirit that overcame men and women, causing them to shout. As Gilmore stated, it was that same shout-generating spirit that inspired people to continue fighting for freedom. They trusted that the Holy Spirit would soon reveal the liberation for which they had hoped.

Historian David D. Daniels says that, since the Civil Rights Movement, African American pentecostalism has contributed to the religious landscape of America in that it has produced political activists and provided platforms for political activists to express the concerns of African American people.⁵³ These activists were deeply religious; they served as political prophets in the liberation of African Americans. They sought to strengthen not only the ethnic culture of African Americans, but also America's larger socio-political cultural context. Their message was directly connected to the gospel message of love and liberation. The leading African American pentecostal church and headquarters for the largest pentecostal-type constituency called the Church of God in Christ – Mason Temple Church of God in Christ -- "served as a focal point of civil rights activities in Memphis during the 1950s and 1960s."⁵⁴

It was on the platform of Mason Temple Church of God in Christ that Martin Luther King, Jr., delivered his last famous speech "I've Been to the Mountaintop," on April 3, 1968. Therefore, it is an act of disrespect to neglect the prophetic nature of the church by refusing to highlight the cultural participation of the African American pentecostal-type church.

Furthermore, pentecostal-type churches were known for cultural affirmation in expressed worship. Daniels suggests that, since the earliest expression of the pentecostal movement in America, the pentecostal-type church has adapted to certain local cultural expressions as evidence of its ability to spread globally. For example, they adapted African expressions such as the ring dance and other practices of spiritual release and manifestations of the Spirit.⁵⁵ This was evident in services for "letting the Spirit have (either) 'Its way in the service,' 'free course,' or 'right of way.'" Partly because of such experiences, C. P. Jones and Charles H. Mason were expelled from the Baptist church, which compelled them to establish a different church, the Church of God in Christ (COGIC.), "where meaningful worship traditions could be preserved, practiced, and produced unencumbered by charges of heathenism or heresy."⁵⁶ Cultural expressions were released from the chokehold of theological condemnation and declared legitimate and adaptable to the gospel such that it gave the Spirit the "right of way" in the service.

A more deliberate willingness to embrace cultural syncretism in worship was the pentecostal movement that swept America in the early twentieth century. Anderson agrees that the pentecostal emphasis on "freedom in the Spirit" was a gift that has rendered the movement inherently flexible in different cultural and social contexts.⁵⁷ Moreover, it is this same gift of cultural flexibility that will allow a Christian renewal in churches for the twenty-first century. Otherwise, freedom in the Spirit within churches and within the missionary nature of the church is restrained by the denial of culture as a theological criterion in shaping and reshaping church doctrine and practice. Consequently, churches would become theologically dry, paranoid and judgmental of cultural nuances that differ from one ethnic group to another (e.g., musical styles and genres, styles of dress and garments).

Pentecostal-type churches hold that the spiritual insight of such passages suggests that women should not wear pants, even if they are designed specifically for women. In Western culture, pants are men's attire. Therefore, "holy attire" should preserve that gender difference.

Additionally, these church leaders do not seem to consider that in the ancient cultures of the passages cited, both men and women wore garments similar to what are today called robes or dresses. There were differences in the design of garments in that culture, just as there are differences in the design of men's and women's pants in Western culture. Therefore, a more reflective understanding and application of the text would suggest that both men and women be permitted to wear the same type of clothing design, as long as this is culturally appropriate.

It is anachronistic to interpret those passages for doctrine of pants for men and robes or dresses and skirts for women. The argument in certain pentecostal-type churches is that, in cultures where women and men wear pants, women should not be allowed to wear pants. Consequently, when women convert to Christianity, they must also adopt the subculture of the church. A woman who is "saved," who turns away from sin toward new life in Christ, must discard pants because they symbolize her former life.

Further, this doctrine prohibits men from wearing skirts, dresses and kilts; implications that primarily affect men's dress in Eastern cultures. In American society, men do not wear such garments. The contradiction in such practices is that, on the one hand, pentecostal-type churches express an anti-cultural understanding of Scripture as it pertains to men's dress in Eastern societies. On the other hand, they uncritically embrace parts of Western culture that do not question male ministers wearing robes for preaching and performing religious rites such as baptisms, weddings and funerals. This issue has caused splits in some pentecostal-type churches and severe discomfort in others, as illustrated in the case study. The narrow imposition of "holy attire" has defined the Church of God, Pillar of the Truth Church in such a way as to prevent women who wear pants and men who wear robes, from entering the church to hear the gospel.

If the gospel is culturally translatable, it cannot be contrary to it, so that when cultural expressions change, church doctrine necessarily adapts to the change. If not, the church risks hindering the spread of the gospel in its attempt to preserve the gospel. The issue of "holy attire" and pentecostal-type churches warrants further study. For example, the topics of "modesty" and "head coverings" are yet being debated among these churches. All these issues reflect the role of culture within biblical hermeneutics as pertaining to the liberation of women. Other culture-related issues such as dancing (e.g., hip-hop, salsa, tap and modern) may be appropriate topics in the reformulation of doctrinal practices, as well.

Furthermore, while I treat the issue of "holy attire" by focusing on the scriptural rationale that prohibits women from wearing pants, my corrective might suffer from a similar cultural superficiality that pervades the doctrinal practice itself. Yet, I take this issue at face value. Although I risk being thought absurd for even discussing this issue, the issue is important. It reflects the extent of problematic doctrinal practices that emerge from poor treatment of the role of culture in biblical hermeneutics. Additionally, "holy attire" presents another oppressive doctrinal practice antithetical to the liberating nature of the gospel. Both issues – hermeneutics and gender oppression -- are important concerns among today's pentecostal-type churches.

African American Cultural Context

Historically, divine sanction of the "Word of God" has been central to pentecostal-type and non-pentecostal-type Protestant churches of the African Diaspora. Limited formal education within pentecostal-type churches, however, gave way to heavy reliance on the Word of God as expressed by spiritual experience, revelations and readings of Scripture. Because of a leader's limited abilities, these experiences, revelations and uncritical biblical readings were interpreted either by intuition or within the context of individual and communal life experiences. Interpreting the "Word of God" became the focus of the preaching moment. In fact, the preaching moment affected every aspect of life. Everything, from healings to business endeavors, to how to live, to what style of music to support, to how one should dress, was dictated through preaching. Preaching remains the essential element of pentecostal-type and non-pentecostal-type Protestant churches of the African Diaspora. Yet, in many cases, preaching and teaching have lacked critical theological methods and critical biblical exegetical skills. Therefore, there is inconsistency in the methodology for theological judgment and, at times, incoherent, doctrinal practices.

Robert M. Franklin, a social ethicist and long-time member of the Church of God in Christ, delineates several items that "everyone should know about black churches." The thirteenth item states, "Black churches are the cultural incubators for several expressions of American genius.... Churches helped to encourage flourishing music styles... Some churches were antagonistic toward 'secular' art forms; however, even those that were born within the church itself [gospel music]."[58] Herein, Franklin identifies an important contradiction in the history of black churches, including Pentecostal-type churches. To remain separate from the world, they safeguarded theological interests from cultural criteria that were uncomfortable for the church.

While the church possessed the gifts of creativity and influence on culture, it became paranoid about losing its sanctity by deliberately embracing culture. Consequently, culture became the pentecostal-type church's enemy and definition of biblical "worldliness," out of which Paul and John called the church.[59] Any cultural appropriation among the church was mainly credited to people who were either not afraid to tread waters of ecclesial heresy, or merely naïve. I say naïve because, although the churches were not voluntarily willing to adapt to culture, they thrived on the cultural traditions within which they were born. Many doctrines produced and adopted were themselves cultural lens through which the church interpreted Scripture. It is naïve to equate culture to the "worldliness" out of which God calls the church, because tone cannot be fully human without standing within one's ethnic, political or social culture.

The gospel has always been effective in the world as it brings the message of hope, healing and salvation, not only into the world, but also within all cultures of the world. This aspect of the pentecostal movement in America is what scholars believe to have attracted the attention of many African Americans. While

European America held African Americans and their cultural expression suspect, the theological authority of Western Christianity influenced mainline black churches. The pentecostal movement welcomed freedom of expression for African Christians so that African descendants felt included without the need to domesticate their so-called "heathenistic" expressions.

Role of Culture in Interpreting Scripture

Culture played an important role in propagating the gospel in the expansion of the early church, in the doctrinal practices perpetuated in the Pauline church, and even much later, in the development of the so-called "Black Church." It is, therefore, important for independent pentecostal-type churches to engage culture as a theological criterion for advancing relevant doctrine and practices for the twenty-first century. In lieu of the esteemed value of Scripture in making theological judgments for doctrinal practice, independent pentecostal-type pastors and theologians must work collaboratively to develop between the academy and the churches mutually critical theological hermeneutics (methods for interpreting Scripture). Clines notes that biblical hermeneutics is helpful not only in the scholarly study of the Bible, but also for the church. Biblical hermeneutics constitutes recognition of the culture-conditioned nature of the Bible and the subsequent impossibility of transferring the Bible and its teachings "neatly" into the contemporary church.[60]

Adopting the "hermeneutic circle" from New Testament scholar Rudolph Bultmann, Latin American theologian Juan Luis Segundo extends hermeneutical methodology for liberation theology. In *The Liberation of Theology*, Segundo defines the "hermeneutic circle" as "the continuing change in our interpretation of the Bible, which is dictated by continuing changes in our present-day reality, both individual and societal."[61]

As used in the practical theological enterprise, the "hermeneutic circle" is a methodology extremely useful to my own emphasis on the "trilateral" (readings of Scripture, experiences of the Holy Spirit and perceptions of culture) for arriving at theological judgments. The "hermeneutic circle" is an appropriate method for interpreting Scripture in light of experiences of the Holy Spirit and perceptions of culture. The resulting interpretation will help to produce more critical doctrine and doctrinal practice for independent pentecostal churches, such as the Rock of Life Church and A Church of God, Pillar of the Truth.

The use of the "hermeneutic circle" requires two pre-conditions: 1) Questions must emerge out of lived experience. Questions rising out of the present are rich enough, general enough, basic enough, and yet relevant enough to change our customary perceptions of Christian life. Only a change in perceptions, or at the very least, a pervasive suspicion about certain doctrinal practices, will enable us to reach the desired critical praxis to force theology back to reality and ask itself new and decisive questions.[62] The main questions are, "What does God require of us?" "Is this doctrinal practice really necessary?" "What are the implications of biblical teachings for contemporary Christian application? and 2) How can Scripture be interpreted in light of lived experience?

If the discipline of theology assumes that it can respond to new questions without changing its customary interpretation of Scripture, that assumption immediately terminates the hermeneutic circle. Therefore, the interpretation of Scripture must change in light of the lived situation.[63] Culture is the shared stories, experiences, language, symbols and patterns of the vernacular in people or groups of people. I argue that, since culture primarily and intricately defines lived situations, it must be held in continuous, critical dialogue with Scripture, to satisfy the preconditions of the hermeneutic circle.

With reference to Scripture, the early church met these preconditions. The early church regarded seriously the contemporary cultures in which the gospel was propagated. It looked to the Hebrew Bible as Scripture. Theologians of the early church, such as the apostle Paul, were not afraid to interpret Scripture for church doctrine in light of the lived experience of the church. Missing from Segundo's interpretation, however, is the role of the Holy Spirit as a guide in making theological judgments for church doctrine and practices. The activity of the Holy Spirit in Jewish and Gentile cultures was a guide to interpreting Hebrew Scripture in the early church. As illustrated above in the discussion of circumcision, Paul interpreted the Hebrew Scriptures in light of culture and the contemporary church. Through this dialogue between Scripture and culture, as guided by experiences of the Holy Spirit, the early church sought to produce and reproduce its own doctrinal practices.

The theological process for Paul and the early church is an antecedent to the "hermeneutic circle" expressed by Segundo. Four decisive factors comprise Segundo's hermeneutic circle. They are relevant to issues of culture at the Rock Church and the issue of culture in A Church of God, Pillar of the Truth's "Affirmation of Faith," and "holy attire." Segundo's "hermeneutical circle" is the following:[64]

1. Experience: Our way of experiencing reality - culture - which leads us to question the doctrinal practice in the first place;

2. Apply ideological suspicion to current doctrinal practice: The application of the "hermeneutic of suspicion" to the methodology for making theological judgments for doctrine and practice;

3. Exegetical Suspicion: A new way of experiencing theological realities that leads to exegetical suspicion that the prevailing interpretation has not taken into account important ideas, concepts, insights or observations;

4. New interpretation of Scripture in light of experience: Our new hermeneutic, our new way of interpreting Scripture, considering other elements of importance.

The new interpretation of scripture must be done in light of experiences of the Holy Spirit and with the element of culture defining the given situation. Consistent with the precedent set by the early church, the contemporary church must engage Scripture in dialogue with culture, guided by the experiences of the Holy Spirit, in making theological judgments for doctrinal practices.

Issue of Changing Cultures

In this chapter, I have discussed the relationship between gospel and culture to support the idea that culture should be taken seriously in making theological judgments for church doctrine. It is, therefore, important to consider that no culture remains frozen. Langdon Gilkey asserts that the gospel is enacted by human subjects in socio-historical situations. He situates the theological enterprise within practical theology because the cultural engagement of the gospel is *praxis-related*.[65] This means that the gospel is interpreted within cultural paradigms. *Praxis* is the critical theological tool that affords the church the theological flexibility to revisit theology, doctrine and practice in light of constantly changing culture. Yet, the power of the gospel subverts culture such that, while culture is adaptable, it does not acquiesce to human standards contrary to its own nature. The church, as required by the nature of the gospel, is called to the critical discovery of balance between critique and affirmation of culture.

In *Theories of Culture,* Kathryn Tanner addresses culture and theology. She argues that Christians are called to liberation. That liberation is adjusted in the course of an ongoing discourse about Christian practice within context.[66] Agreeing with Tanner, I contend that when churches such as the Rock of Life Church closes its theological mind to the celebration of culturally specific events such as Martin Luther King Jr. Day and Heritage Month, they block out the continuing story of the gospel as revealed in the life of African Americans. When a church closes itself to re-interpretations of Scripture used to demonize women for wearing pants, the possibility of utilizing culture as a theological resource in reshaping doctrine is blocked. The gospel is not intrinsically against culture. Therefore, theology and doctrinal practices cannot remain true to the gospel while uncritically opposing culture.

If pentecostal-type churches do not begin to regard cultural change as reasonable grounds for re-examining church doctrine, the pentecostal-type church will gradually become irrelevant. The evolution of cultural perspectives, e.g., those related to women's wearing pants in church, alters the lens through which Scripture can be interpreted. Hence, it is imperative that hermeneutical interpretations take into consideration cultural diversity and historical change.

In developing doctrinal practices at A Church of God, Pillar of the Truth, the question is often posed, "What does the Bible say about this?" My concern is that the formation of the question sounds much like one that a mechanic might ask when diagnosing a problem with a car. He or she might phrase a question similar to the following: "What does the book say about this problem?" The mechanic expects a literal systematic process to fix the problem. Therefore, when the leadership of the church asks the wrong question when asking, "What does the Bible say about this?" This question reduces the Bible to something like a repair manual and the leadership to the role of mechanic. While repair manuals and mechanics are potentially reasonable for functional problems, the problems facing Christian churches face problems of culture, theology, and doctrinal practices that are far more dynamic and unyieldingly reflective.

Moving Forward: Relationship between Culture and Pentecostal-type Churches

Among Bible-based pentecostal churches, the question should no longer be, "What does the Bible *say* about this?" Instead, the question should be, "What does the Bible *mean* by this?" This question avoids the step-by-step literal approach to reading scripture. The question of meaning triggers the need for multiple tenets to aid in the interpretive process. In altering cultural perceptions, important questions arise regarding Scriptural hermeneutics, questions that would invariably affect theological judgments. Tanner argues that Christian theology (church doctrine and practices) must be subject to change. Agreeing with Tanner, I add that church doctrine and practices must also remain committed to the gospel's intrinsic nature of love and liberation. For pentecostal-type churches, love and liberation are normative principles that aid in interpreting Scripture in living contexts.

How is it possible to remain open to change and yet true to the centuries-old concepts of love and liberation intrinsic to the gospel? When we add the Holy Spirit to the equation, we may be closer to the answer we seek. Although Tanner does not elaborate on pneumatological categories and their role in theological matters, she does support the important role the Spirit bears in working with culture, albeit with too limited authority for many churches. She claims that the activity of the Spirit is what links Christians to Judaism—"God's steadfast faithfulness"—and what Christ alone affirms—"God's free grace to Gentiles publicly in Christ."[67] Tanner builds her argument on a reading in Genesis 1, which states that the Spirit moved upon the face of the waters. Her reading of the passage suggests that as the Spirit moved upon the face, and not the depths, of the water, theological judgment among various cultures is guided by shifting waves upon the material surfaces of Christian practices that may link together to form intelligible chains.

As a pentecostal-type theologian, I contend that there is greater depth to the power and role of the Spirit than Tanner acknowledges. In fact, John 3:8 speaks of a birth of the Spirit when it says, "The wind blows where it will and you cannot tell from where it comes and to where is goes, so is everyone who is born of the Spirit." This passage suggests that the Spirit influences persons and communities at a deeper level of lived experience. After applying an *intertextual* exegesis to the Genesis and John passages, it seems reasonable to conclude that the Spirit is largely responsible for the birthing process. In Christian theology, the Holy Spirit works within creation to birth Christian life. Along with the Bible-based theological aspirations, pentecostal-type Christians place heavy emphasis on the role of the Holy Spirit in guiding the life of the congregation, as well as in guiding the everyday life of the Spirit-filled Christian. It is important to note that the activity of the Spirit accompanies cultural perceptions; experiences of the Spirit are central to making sound theological judgments amid changing cultures. The Spirit serves as agent of the gospel to guide in the critique and affirmation of cultural fluctuations. The Spirit therefore assures that the nature of love and liberation enshrined in the gospel is not violated. She makes her revelatory recommendations through a variety of experiences, whether *glossalalia*, visions, dreams, or preaching.

Notes

1. B.A. Mazibuko, *Education in Mission/Mission in Education* (Frankfurt A.M.: Peter Lang, 1987), 346.

2. Nico Botha, "Metaphors and Portrayals of Jesus in New South African And Their Implications for Christian of Missiological Knowledge," *Mission is Crossing Frontiers: Essays in Honour of Bongani A. Mazibuko*(Pietermaritzburg, South Africa: Cluster Publications, 2003), 99.

3. Particularly women, because women's issues in the church are the focus of this book.

4. This doctrine and its subsequent practice resulted from efforts to understand Deuteronomy 22:5, in relation to the prevailing culture.

5. Allan H. Anderson, "The Gospel and Culture in Pentecostal Mission in the Third World," Paper presented at the 9th Conference of the European Pentecostal Charismatic Research Association, Missions Academy, University of Hamburg, Germany, (July 1999), http://www.epcra.ch/papers_pdf/ hamburg/anderson_1999.pdf (accessed 21 December, 2007).

6. Richard H. Niebuhr, *Christ and Culture* (San Francisco: Harper, 2001),65. Examples of zone one include Tertullian, Benedictine Monasticism, Quakers, Mennonites, and Leo Tolstoy.

7. Niebuhr's examples for this zone include the early Gnostics, Abelard, eighteenth-century rationalists such as John Locke, Immanuel Kant, Thomas Jefferson, and liberal theologians such as Albrecht Ritschl.

8. Niebuhr's examples for the third zone include early apologists such as Justin Martyr, Clement of Alexandria, and the medieval theologian, Thomas Aquinas.

9. Niebuhr's fourth zone is best expressed by 16th century reformer, Martin Luther. Christ above culture refers more accurately to a synthesis of "Christ and culture," while "Christ and culture in paradox" implies a sort of dualism, a dissonance in which one strives to change the culture while accepting that culture may not change until Christ returns.

10. Niebuhr locates St. Augustine, John Calvin, and F. D. Maurice as closest to this category.

11. Thomas H. Groome, *Sharing Faith: A Comprehensive Approach to Religious Education and Pastoral Ministry – The Way for Shared Praxis* (New York: HarperCollins Publishers, 1991), 152-153. Groome explains that the term "inculturation" is used

primarily among scholars in the Roman Catholic churches to explain the relationship between faith and culture (see Groome,489). I use it here to support
culture as a theological tenet, along with experiences of the Holy Spirit and Scripture, in the development of a critical formula for practical theology.

12. Michael Goheen, "The Urgency of Reading the Bible as One Story in the Twenty-first Century," (Public Lecture given at Regent College, Vancouver, B.C., Thursday, 2 November 2006), 12.

13. See, Lamin Sanneh, *Translating the Message: The Missionary Impact on Culture* (Mary Knoll: Orbis Books, 1989).

14. II Corinthians 3:17.

15. Galatians 2:4.

16. I Corinthians 12:13; Gal 3:28; Col 3:11.

17. I Timothy 2:12; I Cor. 14: 24-36.

18. See Marvin R. Vincent, *The International Critical Commentary: A Critical and Exegetical Commentary on the Epistles to the Philippians and to Philemon* (Edinburgh: T&T Clark, 1955), 97.

19. Philippians 3:9.

20. Ralph P. Martin, *New Century Bible Commentary: Romans* (Grand Rapids: William B. Eerdmans Publishing Company, 1976), 131.

21. Ibid.

22. Morna D. Hooker, "The Letter to the Philippians," *The New Interpreter's Bible: A Commentary in Twelve Volumes* (Nashville: Abingdon Press, 2000), 527.

23. Perhaps, the struggle between former theological commitments and the full practice of new understanding of the gospel is reflected in Paul's discourse on the law in his mind and the law of God in his inmost self as recorded in Romans 7:21-25. Yet, even in this pericope, Paul is optimistic that in Christ, there is resolution between his new theology and his former religious commitments. This struggle is revealed throughout Paul's ministry as he teaches about the liberating spirit, but fails to practice an ecclesial affirmation of women.

24 I understand that my rendering of "continued revelation" does not find a home among the orthodox theologians.

25. Brad Ronnell Braxton, *No Longer Slaves: Galatians and African American Experience* (Collegeville, MN: The Liturgical Press, 2002).

26. Brad Ronnell Braxton, "The Role of Ethnicity in the Social Location of I Corinthians 7:17-24," in *Yet with a Steady Beat: Contemporary U.S. Afrocentric Biblical Interpretation,* ed. Randall C. Bailey (Atlanta: Society of Biblical Literature, 2003), 29.

27. Ibid.

28. I draw a parallel between these two passages in I Corinthians 12:13. Dennis R. MacDonald agrees with me that Paul, in I Corinthians 12:13, is not emphasizing the abolition of cultural differences, but emphasizing the unity of diverse cultural groups and genders present in one body—the church. See Dennis R. MacDonald, *There is No Male and Female: The Fate of a Dominical Saying in Paul and Gnosticism* (Philadelphia: Fortress Press, 1987), 116.

29. Acts 15.

30. Luke Timothy Johnson, *The Acts of the Apostles: Sacra Pagina Series V5* (Collegeville, MN: Liturgical Press, 1992), 7.

31. Jacob Jervell, *Luke and the People of God: A New Look at Luke-Acts* (Minneapolis: Augsburg Publishing House, 1972), 15.

32. Ibid., 66.

33. Acts 2:6.
34. Acts 2:7-8.
35. Acts 2:11.
36. Lamin Sanneh, *Translating the Message*, 46.
37. Acts 15 and all of Colossians and Galatians.
38. Michael Glass, "The New Testament and Circumcision." *Circumcision Information and Resource Pages* (October 2001), http://www.cirp.org/pages/ cultural/glass1 (accessed 15 March, 2008).
39. Acts 16:3. Paul communicates divine acceptability of a culturally diverse church in his teachings on circumcision in Rom 4:7-17; I Cor 7:17; Gal 5:6; Col 3:11.
40. Galatians 2:3.
41. Martin Luther, Johann Friedrich, Wilhelm Tischer and Samuel Simon Schmucker, *A Commentary on St. Paul's Epistle to the Galatians* (Philadelphia: Quaker City Publishing House, 1872), 200- 202. This source is extremely dated. I have used it here to illustrate the progression of thought over time.
42. Ibid., 202.
43. Hans Dieter Betz, *Galatians: A Commentary on Paul's Letter to the Churches in Galatia* (Philadelphia: Fortress Press, 1979), 89.
44. Ibid.
45. Hans Hubner, *Law in Paul's Thought* (New York: Continuum International Publishing Group, 2004), 21.
46. Lamin Sanneh, *Translating the Message,* 1.
47. Roswith I. H. Gerloff, *A Plea for British Black Theologies: The Black Church Movement in Britain in its Transatlantic Cultural and Theological Interaction* (2 vls.) (New York/ Paris: Peter Lang, 1992), 61.
48. Roswith Gerloff with A. Akrong , *Global Atlas* (Edinburgh Centenary: forthcoming, 2010) (quoted from the unpublished abridged version for print), 3.
49. Ibid. 4.
50. As quoted in William Beardslee (ed.), *The Way Out Must Lead In: Life Histories in the Civil Rights Movement.* 2nd ed. (Westport, CT: Lawerence Hill Publishers, 1983), 144.
51. Luke 4:18-19.
52. David James Randolph, *The Renewal of Preaching* (Philadelphia: Fortress, 1969), 2.
53. David D. Daniels III, "'Doing All the Good We Can': The Political Witness of African American Holiness and Pentecostal Churches in the Post-Civil Rights Era," in *New Day Begun: African American Churches and Civic Culture in Post-Civil Rights America*, R. Drew Smith (ed.), (Durham: Duke University Press, 2003), 164.
54. Mason Temple Church of God in Christ, "We Shall Overcome: Historic Places of the Civil Rights Movement – Mason Temple Church of God in Christ," http://www.nps.gov/nr/travel/civilrights/tn1.htm (accessed 27 December 2007).
55. David D. Daniels III., "The Cultural Renewal of Slave Religion: Charles P. Jones and the Emergence of the Holiness Movement in Mississippi" (Ph.D. Dissertation, Union Theological Seminary, 1992), 185.
56. Cheryl Sanders, *Saints in Exile* (New York: Oxford University Press, 1996), 16.
57. Allan H. Anderson, "The Gospel and Culture in Pentecostal Mission in the Third World," http://www.epcra.ch/ papers_pdf/hamburg/anderson_1999.pdf (accessed 21 December, 2007).

58. Robert M. Franklin, *Crisis in the Village: Restoring Hope in African American Communities* (Minneapolis: Fortress Press, 2007), 113.

59. See Romans 12:2. "Do not be conformed to this world, but be transformed by the renewing of your mind, so that you may discern what is the will of God—what is good and acceptable and perfect." "Therefore, come out from among them, and be separated, says the Lord." 1 John 1:15 "Do not love the world or the things of the world. If anyone loves the world, love for the Father is not with him or her."

60. D.J.A. Clines, "Biblical Hermeneutics in Theory and Practice," *Christian Brethren Review* 31, 32. (1982), 69.

61. Juan Luis Segundo, *The Liberation of Theology* (Mary Knoll: Orbis Books, 1976), 8.

62. Ibid.

63. Ibid., 9.

64. Ibid.

65. Langdon Gilkey, "The Spirit and the Discovery of Truth through Dialogue" *Experience of the Spirit* (New York: Seabury Press, 1974), 59.

66. Kathryn Tanner, *Theories of Culture: A New Agenda for Theology* (Minneapolis: Augsburg Fortress Press, 1997), 163.

67. Ibid., 162.

Chapter 4
The Ordination of Women

Pentecostal-type churches must critically administer theological tenets as a crucial phase in the practical theological enterprise. This means that they should apply the "hermeneutic of suspicion"[1] to doctrinal practices. Accordingly, oppressive doctrinal practices will then be reshaped to conform to the liberating nature of the gospel. The critical trilateral exchange, when systematically administered, should exemplify change in doctrine and doctrinal practices regarding the oppression of women based on the following two mutually dependent premises. First, the Holy Spirit's use of women to proclaim the liberating power of the gospel has been progressive throughout the African Diaspora; and second, interpretations of Scripture that exclude women from proclaiming the gospel must be re-interpreted in light of the liberating power of the Holy Spirit. My trilateral exchange builds upon these premises by interpreting Scripture through the lens of the movement of the Holy Spirit and local culture.

This chapter will address the ecclesial prohibition on the ordination of women. With my trilateral proposal, I argue that experiences of the Holy Spirit critically confer with culture as hermeneutical partners that aid the interpretation of Scripture to shape doctrinal practices that, in turn, uphold the theological liberty and activity of the Spirit and understand the vital function of culture within living faith.[2]

The practice of excluding women from ministry, church leadership, and even from some denominational ecclesial voting processes results from cultural oppression. This deeply rooted oppressive behavior needs critical evaluation as it seems to violate the liberating norms of the gospel.

In this enterprise, I employ the trilateral paradigm to produce a critical theological judgment that liberates women from the exclusion of ordained ministry. This chapter introduces critical dialogue from an international conference for African churches in Berlin, Germany, in 2003. *The African Christian Diaspora Conference* was an event under the auspices of several German universities and the Council of Christian Communities of an African Approach in Europe and looked into the partition of Africa and implications for Christian mission today." A situation at the conference helped to elucidate the theological problems of interpretation and doctrinal practices that prohibit the ordination of women. Finally, this chapter employs a critical treatment of the trilateral paradigm to support the ordination of women at the Rock Church and the Church of God, Pillar of the Truth, as described in Chapter 2.

Controversy at the African Christian Diaspora Conference

The conference, "The Berlin-Congo Conference 1884-The Partitioning of Africa and Implications for Christian Mission Today," was convened in Berlin. The council invited me to present a paper on the situation of African American churches. More than 100 delegates were present. Pastor Johannes Wilson and Archbishop Anna Oku-Adagame were among the delegates who addressed this debate. Pastor Wilson and Archbishop Oku-Adagame are also board members of the Council of Christian Communities of an African Approach in Europe. Both are pastors of pentecostal churches; Wilson is pastor of an independent pentecostal church in northeast Germany, although he is originally from Sierra Leone. Anna Oku-Adagame is Archbishop of Born Again Christ Healing Church International and pastor of the Mission House in Hornsey, London. She is originally from Nigeria.

With complete confidence, Pastor Wilson said, "At creation, God created man first. The man is the head of the woman. God created the man to be the leader. A woman might be able to preach, but she is not supposed to have authority over the man. That is what the Bible says. A woman should not pastor. The man is the head. That is why pastoring is a man's job." The crowd sighed and began to whisper in division. Wilson added, "Look at Jesus' twelve disciples. They were only men. Jesus did not send women to carry out the Great Commission."

When Wilson sat down, Archbishop Oku-Adagame boldly stood up. She said, "Wait a minute! My Lord [though it was not a quote from God but a teaching in Paul][3] said, 'There is neither male nor female.' God can use anybody God wants to and whenever God wants to, if they only submit to God. Hallelujah! What gets me is that people are always saying, 'The Bible said this and the Bible said that.' Tell me, what did the Spirit say? 'The letter kills, but the Spirit gives life.'"[4]

Towards A New Way for Biblical Interpretation

While some pentecostal-type churches have used Scripture and spiritual revelation to carve out a theological position regarding women in ordained ministry, their claims often present contradictions that produce theological train wrecks. I hope to crystallize the problems of incoherent theological methodology and inconsistent theological judgments that emerge from the situation illuminated above.

During the Protestant Reformation, Martin Luther was convinced that the church should make its doctrinal claims *sola scriptura*, and pentecostals have adopted this claim. They have been resistant to questioning the "written Word." Pentecostals, therefore, have been called, "People of the Book."[5] The ambiguity of biblical hermeneutics that emerges from contemporary scholarship, however, forces one to acknowledge that doctrinal practices cannot be based upon Scripture alone. Leaders in pentecostal-type churches are often quoted as saying, "If the Bible said it, I believe it." However, the contemporary genius of biblical hermeneutics informs us that many claims for "what the Bible says" are nothing more than mere interpretations which vary with the interpreter, because all readings of Scripture are filtered through the lens of the interpreter.

Males who interpret Scripture through gender-biased hermeneutics have dominated the history of biblical interpretation, presenting a biblical Christianity that excludes women from ordained ministry. Feminist critiques, such as those of Elizabeth Schüssler-Fiorenza, have uncovered the biases of male-dominated biblical interpretation. She calls for a "remedial and revisionist aim."[6] The "remedial and revisionist aim" advocates for and overthrow of the androcentric bias in biblical interpretations. According to the feminist revisionist, interpreters who have projected androcentric bias onto biblical texts have so patriarchalized them such that the fullness of the Holy Spirit's liberating power that is also intrinsic to the gospel is safeguarded from women. Biblical interpretation must be "depatriarchalized" because, correctly understood, it actually fosters the liberation of women.[7]

It is difficult to interpret "what the Bible says" without considering the historical context within which the Bible was written. It is important for biblical interpretation to note that societies within which biblical texts were born were patriarchal. The issue is not, therefore, simply "what women were or were not allowed to do in the Bible," but rather, whether or not the liberating power of God was present in the early Christian movement, a power that seems to be restrained in the churches of our communities today.

The gospel preached in biblical times was spiritually and ethnically liberating. When one understands the gender constraints on women in early Christian societies, one can more easily recognize the seeds of women's liberation that Christianity brought to those societies. I argue that Paul's comments concerning women in I Timothy 2:11-15 and I Corinthians 11 and 14, were early signs of social change in women's participation in the worship experience. Very few public settings, particularly Jewish settings, would allow the public presence and participation of women with men, except the house churches. The mere fact that women were allowed to learn in I Timothy 2:11, and to lead public prayer in I Corinthians 11, reveals the liberating effects of the gospel upon early Christianity. Many contemporary interpreters are willing to embrace the liberation of Christ from slavery. Yet, as illustrated in the case study, many still struggle to maintain patriarchal control over the liberating power of Christ in regards to ordination. Something in this paradigm seems twisted. Given the evidence of such theological ethics of the gospel *toward* liberating women in early Christianity, the contemporary church may, in fact, be violating the gospel in restricting women from spreading that same gospel through the Church.

Moving Beyond Oppressive Biblical Interpretations

Pentecostal-type churches typically claim a commitment to "what the Bible says." I challenge them to consider the lens through which they read, "What the Bible says." The lens is at times uncritical as to whether a certain biblical claim is for or against ordaining women. An old saying in pentecostal-type church circles is, "The Bible says what it means and means what it says." Michael J. Brown interposes, "...except when it doesn't."[8] Independent pentecostal churches of the African Diaspora have yet to confront the reality that the Bible says no more than what the Bible is interpreted to say.

There is a collage of problems that contribute to the problem of oppressive biblical interpretation. Certain, Eurocentric interpretations of the Bible have also dominated the history of biblical interpretation. As feminist scholars indicate, within Eurocentric interpretations, there are no few problems. These interpretations have impressed upon traditional normative interpretations of scripture. Yet, Eurocentric interpretations cannot bear full burden for continued oppressive interpretations among churches of African Diaspora.

Womanist theologians like Delores Williams in *Sisters in the Wilderness* and elsewhere raises the issue of male clergy attitudes, and African American male attitudes, as a reason why Black Theology is insufficient to redress Black/African American women's experiences of injustice; hence a womanist theology is needed.[9] African scholars such as Ambe J. Njoh and others note that many pre-colonial African societies maintained somewhat parallel male and female pronged chieftaincies.[10] However, in other pre-colonial African societies, men often dominated the chief's court.[11] As non-African influences infiltrated Africa from Islamic societies and European societies, women roles of leadership weakened. It is, however, reasonable to conclude that the shifting of indigenous norm from male and female leadership to male dominated chieftainships planted seeds of greed for male dominance in the African male and remains today in the attitude of the men from the African Diaspora. Perhaps, this transference explains why Eurocentric male dominated biblical interpretations that give precedence to male superiority in church leadership finds resistant lodge in the psyche of African American male clergy, male dominated theologies, ecclesial structures and church doctrine and practice.

In *Cultural Interpretation: Orienting New Testament Criticism,* Brian K. Blount asserts that when scholars include the perspectives of marginal members of society, biblical interpretation can have new meaning. New insights would affect both the academic and ecclesiastical arenas."[12] Blount's notation is particularly important in churches with esteemed reverence for Scripture, i.e., churches of the African Diaspora in general, and pentecostal-type churches, in particular. This means that a different approach to biblical interpretation has revolutionary potential for pentecostal-type churches of the African Diaspora. On the one hand, the revolutionary potential of culture within biblical interpretation could mean the dawn of a new day for biblical scholarship and the contemporary church, because it includes perspectives traditionally excluded. Cultural interpretation has the potential for innovative insight into the "Word of God."

On the other hand, scholars such as Brown are skeptical that African American churches would eagerly embrace this new approach to biblical interpretation. Since there are yet few African American pastors with formal training in biblical criticism, Brown argues, "Biblical interpretation is at the heart of the African American community's present existential plight."[13] Brown explains that many African Americans are reluctant to break away from the fundamentalist interpretation of Scripture, and this fear is what has caused the African American community to become complicit in its own cultural oppression.[14] Based on insight from Brown, I contend that a similar fear among independent pentecostal churches of the African Diaspora contributes to the perpetuation of gender oppression in doctrinal practices. As argued later, biblical interpretations handed over from Eurocentric interpreters and Eurocentric churches have crippled Western theology, and are, perhaps, the invisible foundation of oppressive doctrinal practices among independent pentecostal churches.

Our cultural complicity stems from our theological presuppositions driving our biblical interpretation. Mary Hayter cautions the biblical theologian "If the Bible is to be authoritative in matters of faith and conduct, it must be the Bible rightly interpreted."[15] But we are left to ask and answer for pentecostal-type churches, "what is rightly interpreted"? I have asserted that one must take into account the historical context of the passage; but, one should not make a conclusion based on history alone. As argued in Chapter 3, the passage must be set in dialogue with a contemporary cultural context for localized relevance. This means that all interpretation of Scripture is *hermeneutical*. No interpretation of Scripture is objective, in the literal sense of the word. A responsible reading of Scripture must take seriously the history of the text; the history in the text, including the *sitz em leben*, or the situation of life surrounding the text, and the relevance of the text for contemporary situations. While this argument is fairly commonplace in the academy, the challenge now faced is how to reform biblical interpretation for doctrinal practice in pentecostal-type churches that roots out cultural and doctrinal oppression, yet honors the distinctive values and theological strengths of their tradition.[16]

John Bright asserts that when one selects passages of the Bible that seem to support a favored position over a disfavored position on an issue, one risks offering a weak or incoherent argument in "no more than a vast collection of proof texts which one may call upon by discretion in order to support one's own arguments or refute those of one's opponents. That is a misuse of the Bible's authority."[17] If one chooses to value Scripture at all in the process of making a coherent, theological judgment, one must confront all passages of the Bible concerning the issue. Then, with the guidance of the Holy Spirit, one must interpret the passage in light of the immediate culture of the interpreter and in dialogue with the context of the passage. On the issue of women in the church, the Bible, on one hand, suggests that the woman is subordinate to the man.[18] On the other hand, there is evidence in Scripture that many women held leadership roles among the people of God (i.e., Miriam,[19] Deborah,[20] Esther,[21] Junia,[22] and

Chloe).[23] The main New Testament passage used for women's newfound liberty in Christ is Galatians 3:27-28. When the theological interpreter does not take all relevant passages into consideration, she or he risks misguided interpretations rendering theological judgments that may be antithetical to the liberating power of the gospel.

Cultural Imperialism

In *Clergy Women: An Uphill Calling*, Zikmund, Lummis and Chang assert that in the late twentieth century, holiness and pentecostal-type denominations were ideologically linked to southern (Eurocentric) religion, with its biblical literalism and resistance to the ordination of women to pastoral ministry.[24] Ada Maria Isasi-Diaz makes a comparable analysis to the one I make here. In *Mujerista Theology*, she explains five faces of oppression among Latinas. The fourth face of oppression, which she calls "cultural imperialism," [25] is relevant to the oppression of African American preaching women. Cultural imperialism occurs when prominent social structures render less dominant experiences or cultures invisible. Isasi-Diaz explains that "cultural imperialism" means that the dominant group projects its own experience as the norm in society and the less dominant group is considered deviant and inferior.[26] Moreover, in the case of African American women preachers, despite their effectiveness in ministry, they are 1) African American and 2) women - "double jeopardy."

When African American men became powerful in the Black Church, they perpetuated the oppression of women inherited from indigenous misogyny and the dominant structures of Euro-America. The adaptation of these norms may, in part, be responsible for resistance to the ordination of women in the Black Church. Nonetheless, permitting women to speak but prohibiting their ordination rendered the church guilty of gender oppression, or, in Isasi-Diaz's parlance, "cultural imperialism" as well as cultural oppression.

Furthermore, the ideological superstructures inherited by pentecostal-type churches from mainline Euro-American denominations have become ecclesiological strongholds in the churches that splintered from those traditions. As a result, the pentecostal movement in America, extending through pentecostal-type churches of the African Diaspora that prohibit women from ordained ministry, contradicts a history of advocating theologies of God's love and the liberating power of the Holy Spirit. This contradiction results in a failure to counter European theologies that restrained African Americans from social equalities, as is also evident in the prohibition of women from ordained ministry during the inception and thriving years of pentecostalism. Throughout the twentieth century, beyond Azusa Street, history shows evidence of how the Holy Spirit worked through women in the growth of pentecostal-type and other churches. Therefore, the injustice created by denying ordained ministry to these women certainly cannot be explained by the experiences of the Holy Spirit. Millions of people have been delivered, discipled, convicted and converted through the preaching of both men and women.

Examples of Ordained, Spirit-filled American Women in Ministry

In the Trilateral that I proffer, experiences of the Holy Spirit continues to guide the church, helping it to overcome the biases of the past, whether they were imposed upon it by an external source, or they have arisen internally through antecedent indigenous practices, or any combination of these sources. Many times, in the broad spectrum of the church, the Holy Spirit manifests experientially among women, calling them and charging them to preach the gospel. As a result, God has used women in unprecedented ways. Converse to the norm, there have been women throughout African American history who were ordained and were quite effective in ministry. Their work in spreading the gospel, establishing churches, and nurturing congregations, has been less noticed, less recognized and less celebrated. If the concern is what God is doing among people through Spirit-filled or pentecostal-type churches, the names of numerous women must rise to the top of the list.

Sojourner Truth, born Isabella Baumfree (1797-1883), was born an American slave. On June 1, 1843 was a life-changing day for Isabella Baumfree. She felt overwhelmed of the Holy Spirit and led to change her name to Sojourner Truth. Then, she set out to travel, preaching the gospel with a message against slavery and a message of gender equality. She told her friends, "The Spirit calls me, and I must go."[27] She quickly became known as a remarkable preacher. She was even more bold and effective as an abolitionist than many of her male counterparts, some of whom she encouraged along the way. Sojourner Truth's influence was notable and dubbed "miraculous" from the "underground railroad" -- though which she freed thousands of slaves -- to Washington D.C. -- where in 1864 she met with President Abraham Lincoln about improving the conditions for African Americans.[28]

Amanda Smith (1837-1915), a Spirit-filled, African American woman evangelist, traveled from the United States to South Africa, Liberia and India preaching and discipling new converts. Smith testifies to a religious experience through which God called her and charged her to go preach the gospel. Adrienne Israel states that Smith was responsible for initiating the message of "sanctification" among African Methodist Episcopal churches in the northeastern United States.[29] She had gifts that attracted listeners to hear her preach the Word of God. An observer, who was present at one of Smith's services at the Mountain Lake Park Camp Meeting in Maryland, recalls, "The pressure for seats in, around and near the pulpit was almost crushing… Until after ten o'clock, this gifted and holy woman of God poured out her bright brain and loving heart on that audience…The crowd lingered to the late closing. It was impossible to make room for an altar service."[30]

In her own autobiography, Smith recalls that when she preached, "the fire seemed to fall on all the people."[31] Perhaps, "the fire" (presumably, Smith is speaking of the Holy Spirit) was free to fall because there was openness to women's leadership and to hearing the gospel through the voice of women.

Israel notes, "Smith's career developed out of the black religious heritage from the era of slavery, trends among Methodists, the late-nineteenth-century holiness revival, and the temperance movement, all of which either directly or indirectly encouraged public leadership roles for women."[32]

Born in Hazlehurst, Georgia, in 1891, by 1925, Ida Bell Robinson became one of the first known African American female bishops. She founded the pentecostal church, Mt. Sinai Holy Church of America. Bishop Robinson testified that during prayer, the Holy Spirit spoke to her to "Come out on Mt. Sinai and loose the women."[33]

Harold Dean Trulear, in his article entitled "Ida B. Robinson: The Mother as Symbolic Presence," captures the motherly nature of the office of pastor.[34] In his description of Robinson, he highlights the appropriateness of her being female in the office of bishop. He says, "The concept of church birthing, in contrast to church building, is consistent with the mother symbol of Ida B. Robinson, and with the notion of life affirmed in the black religious tradition."[35] According to Trulear, this metaphor of birthing and mothering churches was the driving force behind Robinson's concern with issues relating to the quality of life. The mother symbol for the office of "pastor" helped Pastor Robinson to structure her church. She avoided the tendency to reduce church leadership to organizational management and institutional maintenance.[36] Through the metaphor of her gender, she was compelled to nurture persons, with specific attention to the development of mature individuals in both the personal and communal spheres. Concisely stated, Rev. Robinson was pastor as mother. She understood new converts as new children to be reared in holiness. After every sermon, she would sing her theme song: "This is the church of Mt. Sinai. Oh, you can't join it. You've got to be born in it. This is the church of Mt. Sinai."[37] According to Trulear, for the members of the Mt. Sinai Holy Churches of America, these mothering qualities and the birthing image helped to cultivate the good life for individuals within the Mt. Sinai Holy Churches and the community life of people in these churches.[38]

The stories of Sojourner Truth, Amanda Smith, and Ida Robinson and their legacies as evangelists and pastor/bishop, alone are only a few examples of the impact that women have made in recent Christian History in America. To borrow from the language of Trulear, the historicity of these and other stories requires deeper "investigation, their complexity mandates analysis, and their efficacy pleads for imitation."[39] These illustrations are important to a theological interpretation or "gospel" reading of African American church history.

African American culture has always benefited from the support, teaching, and preaching of both men and women. Based on this reality, it is counterintuitive to silence the voice of a particular gender. Yet, there is a blatant disconnect between historical evidence of the effectiveness of women's preaching throughout the world and pentecostal-type church doctrines that restrict women from ordained ministry. There is, therefore, a need for a culturally-specific acknowledgement and theological interpretation of what God has done and is doing among pentecostal-type African American people.

Many African American women have proved their charismatic leadership skills and effectiveness in preaching. In addition, several accounts within African American history indicate where people have benefited in their spiritual walk or Christian journey from women evangelists and pastors. For example, we rarely hear of roles women have played in the spiritual experience of black enslavement. Many enslaved women preached the gospel during worship services held on plantations.[40] Their roles as preachers helped to sustain the day-to-day spiritual life of these oppressed persons.[41]

By the end of the eighteenth century and during the great religious revival era of camp meetings, when Freewill Baptists, Christian Connection, and Methodists allowed women to preach and exhort more freely than before; women preachers emerged in large numbers. Between 1800 and 1845, women preachers in several denominational churches were accepted as evangelists, but not as ordained ministers. The male-dominated hierarchical structures of the "Black Church" were torn between the effectiveness of women ministers and their own inadequate, theologically-justified, cultural structures of power and dominance. These women were gradually freed to preach from the pulpits of many black churches;[42] yet, the prominent social structures (European-America) that prohibited the liberation of women in society may have also influenced the ecclesiology of the "Black Church" thereby contributing to the "Black Church's" reluctance to ordain it's preaching women.

While the dominant structures of society limited women's leading roles in the propagation of the gospel, there were yet illustrations of European-American women as well as the African American women that persevered against the odds of male-dominated societal structures and church leadership, proving effective in spreading the gospel. Phoebe Palmer (1807-1874) is a good example of a preaching woman who helped to spread the Holiness tradition. Palmer and her husband Walter Palmer served as itinerant preachers, receiving an abundance of invitations from churches, conferences, and camp meetings. Although Walter Palmer spoke at these meetings, Phoebe became more popular as a preacher and became well-known for her significant role in spreading the concept of Christian holiness throughout the United States and the rest of the world. She wrote several books, including *The Way of Holiness*, which was a foundational book in the Holiness movement.[43] Also, Antoinette Brown Blackwell (1825-1921) who served in social ministry. Blackwell was a minister whose calling was to the broken and marginalized of society. She was an unshakeable force and profoundly courageous advocate for the underprivileged, the abolition of slavery, and women's rights. She was also pioneering female suffragists in the U.S. By September 15, 1853, the First Congregational Church in Butler and Savannah, New York ordained Antoinette the first woman minister of a recognized denomination in the United States. Antoinette's ministry as advocate included her historic influence in a letter to President Theodore Roosevelt, urging him to support the federal suffrage amendment.[44]

Women in African American Church History

During the pentecostal movement of the early twentieth century, half the twelve elders at the Azusa Street Mission who delegated and ordained missionaries and evangelists were women. Estrelda Alexander records that some of the preaching women of Azusa Street were African American women such as Ophelia Wiley, Lucy Farrow, and Jennie Evans.[45] According to Alexander, women were involved in every aspect of spreading the gospel. They exhorted, preached, served on administrative boards, helped edit and publish the newspaper, and helped maintain the mailing lists that supported the church. While the larger society was still wrestling with the issue of women's "rightful place," the women associated with the spread of pentecostalism found freedom to express their calling and leadership gifts in the African American pentecostal church. Many mainline denominations, influenced by Euro-centric theology, were reluctant to ordain women; however, women associated with the pentecostal movement at Azusa Street claimed their own ordination by God through the power and revelation of the Holy Spirit (even when male leadership of the churches used their gifts to build their churches but refused to ordain them). They pounded the pulpits, proclaiming the Word of God and making converts and disciples everywhere they went throughout the world.[46]

Thousands of people, mostly African Americans, from the African Diaspora were baptized in the Spirit at the Azusa Street Mission. Tensions grew between Euro-American pentecostals and African American pentecostals, largely over emotive expressions ---forms of dance and vocal outbursts. Partially because of these alleged Afrocentric expressions, C.P. Jones and Charles H. Mason were forced to establish what became known as the leading African American pentecostal-type church----the Church of God in Christ (C.O.G.I.C.), "where meaningful worship traditions could be preserved, practiced, and produced unencumbered by charges of heathenism or heresy."[47]

While Mason resisted the cultural imperialism of Eurocentric theology that sought to oppress Afrocentric emotive expressions in worship, he failed to challenge theologies that oppressed women by excluding of them from ordained leadership in the church. Until today, this leading African American pentecostal headquarters, Mason Temple Church of God in Christ, of Memphis, Tennessee, continues to prohibit the ordination of women. It seems fitting that a movement which takes seriously the experience of the Holy Spirit to cause "sons and daughters to prophesy (proclaim)"[48] "liberty to those who are wounded"[49] would not only apply that liberating experience of the Holy Spirit to its liberating liturgical categories of the church, but also to its gender-oppressive hierarchical structure and doctrinal practices.

Holy Spirit and Culture as
Theological Bedfellows

Pentecostal-type churches of the African Diaspora must maintain a dual consciousness—as a cultural community and a pentecostal community. As argued previously, the gospel is not against culture *per se*. Therefore, an integral relationship between faith and culture must be understood dynamically. Christian theology and doctrinal practices cannot remain true to the Christian faith if they are in opposition to the cultural affinity intrinsic in the gospel. As argued in the previous chapter, there is no purely Christian theology devoid of cultural sensitivities. Any claims of an "uncultural" Christian theology contradict the very nature of the gospel and, as such, are antithetical to the essence of the Christian faith. Paul Tillich asserts, "Religion is the substance of a culture; culture is the form of religion."[50] I understand Tillich to mean that the Christian faith is expressed by the cultural context of its adherents. The cultural context impresses upon the Christian faith as the faith also impresses upon cultural contexts.

Gilkey asserts that "'an 'uncultural' and so absolute statement of the gospel is, in fact, a cultural statement of the gospel from another time parading before our modern eyes as an eternal, changeless and so definitive statement."[51] Agreeing with Gilkey, I believe that an "uncultural" claim on the gospel actually causes much of the "cultural imperialism" argued above. Biblical interpretations that lack a localized[44] cultural hermeneutic has resulted in decades of misapplication of a liberating gospel. One means of correcting such a misapplication of the gospel is for the church to take into account the practical effectiveness of women's leadership from the first century of the early church all the way through the effective leadership of women in the twenty-first century pentecostal-type churches.

Developing leadership in the Church has involved the expanding proclamation of the gospel which therefore required even the early Church to culturally interpret the theological liberating power of the gospel. So too, God has revealed the liberating gospel in culture through the activity of the Holy Spirit and unique spiritual experiences of women's leadership.

In "The Pentecostal Movement," Margaret Poloma asserts that part of the legacy of pentecostal-type churches is that, through experiences of the Holy Spirit, there is a God-human encounter. She rightly describes this encounter as one of perceived "intimacy with the divine,"[52] whereby God is able to reveal God's will for humans and share with them revelations concerning their immediate lives and their future. Rodney Starks understands this God-human encounter as a marriage between theological tenets of the activity of the Holy Spirit and culture. Starks calls the revelatory encounter between God and humanity a dyadic interaction wherein God and persons are actors in social encounter. I understand this to mean that God locates God's self in culture as God communicates with the individual. By entering culture, God affirms peoples' cultural locations as God speaks in language, signs, and symbols to communicate with people. Stark designates four categories of this social encounter:

1. The human actor simply notes (feels, senses, etc.) the existence or presence of the divine actor.

2. Mutual presence is acknowledged; the divine actor is perceived as noting the presence of the human actor.

3. The awareness of mutual presence is replaced by an affective relationship akin to love or friendship.

4. The human actor perceives himself or herself as confidant of and/or a fellow participant in action with the divine actor.[53]

From these categories of the divine-human encounter, we see that as mutual presence is acknowledged, the role of culture in the encounter is part of our experience and understanding of God (the theological enterprise). The presence of God in one's life is affirmed while, simultaneously, the presence of God affirms the individual in the midst of culture. Pentecostal-types believe that after Jesus ascended, God sent the Holy Spirit to sustain this divine-human encounter.

Because pentecostal-type churches also highly value Scripture, they struggle with the God-human social encounter and the call of God to overcome worldly commitments or cultural conflicts. Phrased in the words of a familiar Scripture, how can we be "*in* the world but not *of* the world?" Charges of relativity often emerge. However, the desired dynamic at play is more so the dialogue between perceptions of culture and the activity of the Holy Spirit or the sensibility of the dual consciousness of the pentecostal-type Christian that provides the hermeneutical lens through which Scripture is interpreted for the relevant, meaningful, critical, transformative, and subversive nature of the gospel.

Holy Spirit and Scripture as Theological Bedfellows

Certainly, conversations on the activity of the Holy Spirit are not foreign to pentecostal-type churches. In fact, the experience of the Holy Spirit is central to the pentecostal-type experience. I have argued that pentecostal-type churches of the African Diaspora must embrace culture as a theological criterion to aid in the interpretation of Scripture for a reshaped church doctrine and practice. However, as pertaining to theological and doctrinal matters, cultural perspectives alone are insufficient for theological judgments. Gilkey adds that the answer to the speculation on the relativity of the gospel must be found in understanding the activity of the Holy Spirit.[54] Gilkey is correct that the Holy Spirit speaks its word *in* and *through* dialogue between church (theology and Scripture) and culture(s) out of which theological reflection and evolving practices (*praxis*) arises.[55] Gilkey further states that Jesus' promise, that the Holy Spirit would remain present in the community to guide it into truth (John 16:13) means that the Holy Spirit will continuously illumine the gospel in the community's life.[56] The relevant question is "What is the Spirit saying?" This question is essential to the theological interpretation of the gospel in dialogue with culture for devising doctrinal practices. In other words, experiences of the Holy Spirit engage culture in the practical theological enterprise for reshaping pentecostal-type church doctrine.

In his article, "The Spirit and Doctrinal Development" Shane Clifton makes the important point that pentecostalism in America emerged out of a critique of "dead traditionalism." This openness to the new things of the Spirit, moreover, should stimulate, as well as inform, pentecostal-type doctrinal reflection for subsequent doctrinal practices.[57] Yet, while some pentecostal-type churches (often called Spirit-filled churches) have valued the prophetic, liberating power of the Holy Spirit *toward* social liberation, many of them have not utilized the experience of the Holy Spirit to liberate women from the oppressive hierarchical structures of the church.

Often pentecostal theology presents conflicts between the activity of the Holy Spirit and readings of Scripture – both of which are central tenets to pentecostal-type theology. Conflicting tenets means that the interpretation of Scripture excludes women from pastoral ministry, yet, women continually appeal to the tradition's theological tenets and contend that the Holy Spirit has revealed to them, the calling of God on their lives to serve in pastoral ministry. Debates within these circles often end in "the battle of the Scriptures." One the one hand, the interlocutor who supports the exclusion of women from ministry, quotes Scripture to support such claim. On the other hand, the interlocutor who supports the inclusion of women in ministry quotes Scripture to override the quoted passages represented by the opposition. Yet, seldom does it seem that these discourses grapple with the tensions in the text for greater insight or clarity in understanding Scripture and the revelations of the Holy Spirit together without creating wars between the two.

This uncritical exchange of competing Scriptural citations is precisely the issue illustrated in the narration cited above at the Berlin Conference. Archbishop Oku-Adagame's claim that the Holy Spirit supports her call to ministry is consistent with my argument for Spirit-guided interpretation of Scripture (in light of cultural perceptions) in the previous chapter. However, her argument is weak. It demonstrates, in part, the problem identified in this book – incoherent and contradicting claims on the trilateral (Scripture, the Holy Spirit, and culture).

The Archbishop's argument reveals an emotional, rather than a critical theological, response to the issue. Initially, she quotes Paul: "There is neither male nor female," as she uses Scripture to argue against the use of Scripture: Next, she uncritically issues a cavalier dismissal of Scripture, "What gets me is that people are always saying, 'The Bible says this and the Bible says that.' Tell me, what does the Spirit say? 'The letter kills, but the Spirit gives life.'" Oddly enough, the Archbishop appears to use what Scripture teaches about the Spirit to dismiss Scripture. So, like the uncritical, misogynistic manipulation of Scripture to prohibit women's ordination, the Archbishop is caught in the same problem as Pastor Wilson's citation of Scripture restricting women's leadership. Both arguments fail to uphold a trilateral reading of conflicting scriptural texts, with experiences of the Holy Spirit and culture.

My own theological analysis supports the Archbishop's desire to affirm the ordination of women based on theological tenets important to her own pentecostal-type constituency. I believe, however, that her argument lacks critical, theological reflection between Scripture and experience for shaping doctrinal practices. My efforts in this book, therefore, are to provide theologically critical, coherent, and systematic criteria that bring together the tenets of primary importance to pentecostal-type churches—Scripture, the Holy Spirit and culture. These tenets can then be used to reinterpret experience with the gospel message, and therefore reshape doctrinal practices that otherwise oppress, instead of liberate, people.

With these criteria and the suggested practical theological methods herein, the Archbishop could make a stronger case by confronting the difficult passages with their traditional interpretations. She could make a more critical, coherent re-interpretation of Scripture for a theology that supports the ordination of women in ministry without creating competing tenets of Scripture and the Holy Spirit. Of course, this dynamic cannot be narrowly relegated to claims made by women seeking ministerial leadership. The conflict is between the theological tenets themselves and is more evident in ecclesial practices prohibiting women's leadership. I contend, however, that if all the tenets are to remain authoritative for doctrinal practices, there must be a more critical, productive means of holding them together or of re-formulating methods to transform doctrinal practices. In this way, church leaders would be better equipped to make theological judgments consistent with the activity of the Spirit and a gospel of love and liberation.

Activity of the Holy Spirit

Traditionally, pentecostal Christians speak of the "Baptism of the Holy Spirit." The language of "Spirit Baptism" or "Baptism of the Spirit" is lifted from biblical references[58] and applied to the spiritual or religious experience associated with speaking in tongues, mystical piety (trance, visions, dreams, dancing, healing and other kinds of religious experiences), and the millennial fervor (apocalypticism and eschatological orientation).[59] Scripture is also used to interpret religious experiences and to predict forthcoming experiences.[60] Neo-pentecostal Christians, however, critique the notion of speaking in tongues as initial evidence of "Holy Spirit Baptism." Generally, neo-pentecostal churches are those that embrace speaking in tongues as *one* of the possible manifestations of the Spirit; however, they generally argue that speaking in tongues is not essential to "Spirit-baptism." Neo-pentecostals base their belief on observations that some Christians are spiritual without the experience of ever speaking in tongues.[61] By critiquing the classical-pentecostal churches' doctrinal practice of "initial evidence," the neo-pentecostal doctrinal practices include other spiritual gifts as evidence of Spirit-baptism. The expansion of these practices and theological interpretation of spiritual baptism offer greater opportunities for more ecumenical dialogue.

However, while the notation is warranted, I am not primarily concerned with the issue of "initial evidence" or the issue of "ecumenism." My argument specifically advances an approach to biblical interpretation for doctrinal practices that dialogue critically with the experience of the Holy Spirit and culture as hermeneutical lens through which the Word of God is discerned more effectively as the liberating gospel. Methodologically, neo-pentecostals, in part, demonstrate my proposition concerning the role of the experiences of the Spirit for theological judgments in reshaping doctrinal practices for independent Pentecostal churches of the African Diaspora. My proposal, however, critiques both classical pentecostal and neo-pentecostal approaches to the relationship between readings of Scripture and experiences of the Holy Spirit.

The experience of the Holy Spirit itself in the New Testament was vital to reinterpreting readings of Hebrew Scripture in light of the gospel and cultural encounters. A case in point is Acts 2:16. After the *glossalalic* episode at Pentecost, Peter immediately interprets Joel 2:28 through the lens of the *glossalalic* experience of the Holy Spirit. Another example is in Acts 15. The Gentiles experienced the outpouring of the Holy Spirit without the prerequisite of circumcision. The Jewish apostles then revisited circumcision in Hebrew Scripture and reinterpreted it in light of the activity of the Holy Spirit. Scripture should not, therefore, be the only hermeneutical lens through which we interpret religious experience. Even the direction of interpretation flows both ways. The experiences of the Holy Spirit (along with culture, as argued in chapter 2) are hermeneutical resources through which all of Scripture is interpreted for a more critical understanding of God's will for the church and its doctrinal practices.

Proposed Symbolic Reading of the "Baptism of the Holy Spirit"

I wish to argue for a symbolic reading of "Spirit baptism." Amos Yong advances a "symbolic" reading of the "Spirit" of pentecostal spirituality in *Discerning the Spirit(s)*. Yong's argument for a symbolic reading of the activity of the Holy Spirit builds on a proposal in Harvey Cox's *Fire from Heaven*. He argues that pentecostalism "may be part of the upsurge of a common human religiosity that is also that undercurrent to the efflorescence of ecstatic and indigenous faith traditions worldwide."[62]

Yong further explains that the activity of the Holy Spirit among pentecostals is *symbolic* of the workings of the Spirit globally, *toward* producing a theology of religions. For Yong, the global upsurge of pentecostalism, therefore, points *toward* (in a symbolic manner) a return to primal spirituality proposed by Cox. Using the global experience of pentecostalism as the hermeneutical lens through which he reads Scripture, Yong interprets biblical texts on the liberty of the Spirit to speak to a possible presence of the Spirit among other religions.

In my argument for the experience of the Holy Spirit in theological judgments, I draw from Yong's symbolic readings of the activity of the Holy Spirit; however, I wish to advance a different symbolic reading. While Yong is interested in the global, inter-religious implications of the symbolisms of pentecostal spirituality, I am interested in a symbolic reading of the "baptism of the Holy Spirit." Baptism of the Holy Spirit is a central experience of the Spirit among pentecostal-type churches (whether or not they subscribe to the doctrine of "initial evidence"). The "baptism of the Holy Spirit," as initiation into the church, offers strong symbolic implications for pentecostal-type theology and doctrinal practices. The symbolic implications are immersed in the experience of the Holy Spirit. Appealing to traditional pentecostal rhetorical authority in "the Bible says" is not sufficient. Many traditional readings of Scripture are oppressive and perpetuate repressive messages antithetical to the liberating nature of the gospel. In short, traditional interpretations of Scripture, along with doctrinal practices, must undergo a symbolic "baptism of the Spirit," which is to argue for a hermeneutic of the activity of the Spirit for contextual theological meaning.

When we adhere to the activity of the Holy Spirit for its symbolic implications, we discover that not only are those experiences creative and supernatural manifestations for individual and communal piety, they are also phenomena with profound implications for the practical theological enterprise in a reshaped church. The salient question that emerges is: "What is the Spirit saying to us?" This means that the activity of the Holy Spirit becomes increasingly critical in discovering clear and relevant meaning of Scripture for doctrinal practice. Through the experiences of the Holy Spirit, God communicates messages that aid in the re-interpretations of Scripture and culture in harmony with the liberating gospel.

In Luke 4:18-20, the activity of the Lord (Holy Spirit) descends upon Jesus with full sensitivity to the situation of oppressed people. The Holy Spirit anoints Jesus to liberate marginalized people from oppressive situations. If pentecostalism takes seriously the activity of the Holy Spirit as the tradition has claimed for more than one hundred years, then churches born into the tradition must embrace the workings of the Holy Spirit within doctrinal practices. These practices are not only concerned with personal piety and communal faith claims (pentecostal-charismatic or pentecostal-type faith communities), but are also committed to the liberating social agency of the gospel. As explained earlier, all of the tenets of the trilateral are essential to theological judgments for generating church doctrine and polity. Therefore, the full trilateral must work together to shape and reshape church doctrine.

Notes

1. The "hermeneutic of suspicion" repudiates exclusionary practices as it propels the theological enterprise towards doctrine better reflective of the libratory nature of the gospel. Edward Farley, *Theologia: The Fragmentation and Unity of Theological Education* (Philadelphia: Fortress Press, 1983), 166. Also, see Juan Luis Segundo, *The Liberation of Theology* (Mary Knoll: Orbis Books, 1976), 9.

2. Luke 4:18-20 speaks to the liberating mission of Christ, a liberating character endowed by the Spirit of the Lord. – The Spirit of the Lord is upon me, because she has anointed me … to liberate the captives. Also, in II Corinthians 3:17, Paul explains the liberating nature of the Spirit – The Lord is that Spirit and where the Spirit of the Lord is, there is liberty.

3. Often church leaders who believe that the Bible is the inerrant, infallible Word of God reference all Scripture as if God wrote it. So, when the bishop says, "My Lord Said," she has no problem alluding to the words of Paul as though they are the words of Jesus.

4. See, II Corinthians 3:6.

5. W. Ma, "Biblical Studies in the Pentecostal Tradition: Yesterday, Today, and Tomorrow," in *Globalization of Pentecostalism: A Religion Made to Travel*; M. W. Dempster, B.D. Klaus, D. Petersen (eds.) (Carlisle, CA: Regnum Books International, 1999), 54. Also, for the language "People of the Book," see L. G. McClung Jr., "Missiology," S. M. Burgess and G. B. McGee (eds.), *Dictionary of Pentecostal and Charismatic Movements* (Grand Rapids: Zondervan Publishing House, 1988), 607.

6. Elizabeth Schüssler-Fiorenza, *But She Said: Feminist Practices of Biblical Interpretation* (Boston: Beacon Press, 1992), 21.

7. Ibid., 23.

8. Michael J. Brown, W*hat They Don't Tell You: A Survivor's Guide to Biblical Studies* (1st ed.) (Louisville: Westminster John Knox, 2000), 66.

9. See, Delores Williams. *Sisters in the Wilderness: The Challenge of Womanist God-Talk* (Mary Knoll: Orbis Books, 1993).

10. Ambe J. Njoh, *Tradition, Culture and Development in Africa: Historical Lessons for Modern Development Planning* (Aldershot: Ashgate Publishing, 2006), 103.

11. Ibid.

12. Brian K. Blount, *Cultural Interpretation: Orienting New Testament Criticism* (Minneapolis: Fortress Press, 1995), 3.

13. Michael J. Brown, *Blackening of the Bible: The Aims of African American Biblical Scholarship* (New York: Trinity Press International, 2004), 161.

14. Ibid.

15. Mary Hayter, *The New Eve in Christ* (Grand Rapids: William B. Eerdmans Publishing Company, 1987), 2.

16. Nico Botha explores a similar notion of biblical interpretation that translates the liberating gospel of Jesus Christ into relevant liberating elements within the South African context. For more on Botha's thesis, see Nico Botha, "Metaphors and Portrayals of Jesus in New South African And Their Implications for Christian of Missiological Knowledge," *Mission is Crossing Frontiers: Essays in Honour of Bongani A. Mazibuko*(Pietermaritzburg, South Africa: Cluster Publications, 2003), 78-102.

17. John Bright, *The Authority of the Old Testament* (London: SCM Press, 1967), 41, 47.

18. Genesis 3:16, I Corinthians 11:2-16 and I Corinthians 14: 33ff.

19. Exodus 15: 20-26.
20. Judges 4-5.
21. Book of Esther.
22. Romans 16:7.
23. I Corinthians 1:11.
24. Barbara Brown Zikmund, Adair T. Lummis and Patricia M. Y. Chang, *Clergy Woman: An Uphill Calling* (Louisville: Westminster John Knox Press, 1998).
25. Ada Maria Isasi-Diaz, *Mujerista Theology: A Theology for the Twenty-first Century* (Mary Knoll: Orbis Books, 1996), 113. As contemplated earlier, cultural imperialism or Eurocentric interpretations may not entirely the problem among African American churches. Yet, it is certainly part of the issue similar to the argument explained in Isasi-Diaz's Mujerista Theology.
26. Ibid.
27. http://www.aoc.gov/cc/art/truth_bust.cfm (accessed 17 May 2009).
28. Ref. Oliver Gilbert and Sojourner Truth, *The Narrative of Sojourner Truth* (Kindle Edition) (Old LandMark Publishing, 2006).
29. Adrienne M. Israel, *Amanda Berry Smith* (Lanham: Scarecrow Press, 1998), 51.
30. "Mountain Lake Park," *Christian Standard*, (23 July 1891), 5.
31. Amanda Berry Smith, *Autobiography: The Story of the Lord's Dealings with Mrs.Amanda Smith, the Colored Evangelist* (1893) (Chicago: Afro-American Press, Division of Afro-American Books, 1969), 112
32. Israel, *Amanda Berry Smith*, 3.
33. Harold Dean Truler, "Ida B. Robinson: The Mother as Symbolic Presence",James R. Goff and Grant Wacker (editors), *Portraits of a Generation: Early Pentecostal Leaders* (Fayetteville: University of Arkansas Press, 2002), 313.
34. Ibid., 309-324.
35. Ibid., 314.
36. Ibid., 315.
37. Ibid.
38. Ibid.
39. Ibid., 324.
40. C. Eric Lincoln and Lawrence H. Mamiya, *The Black Church in the African American Experience* (Durham: Duke University Press, 1990), 270-280.
41. Adrienne M. Israel, 3.
42. Ibid.
43. For more on Phoebe Palmer, see Charles Edward White. *The Beauty of Holiness: Phoebe Palmer as Theologian, Revivalist, Feminist, and Humanitarian* (Zondervan/Francis Asbury Press, 1986). Phoebe Palmer, *The way of holiness,: with notes by the way; being a narrative of religious experience resulting from a determination to be a Bible Christian.* New York: Printed for the author, 1854, Ann Arbor, Michigan: University of Michigan Library, 2005. Antoinette Brown Blackwell (1825-1921) was a minister whose calling was to the broken and marginalized of society. She was an unshakeable force and profoundly courageous advocate for the underprivileged, the abolition of slavery, and women's rights. She was also pioneering female suffragists in the U.S. By September 15, 1853, the First Congregational Church in Butler and Savannah, New York ordained Antoinette the first woman minister of a recognized denomination in the United States. Antoinette's ministry as advocate included her historic influence in a letter to President Theodore Roosevelt, urging him to support the federal suffrage amendment.

44. For more on Antoinette Brown, see Elizabeth Cazden. *Antoinette Brown Blackwell: A Biography*. Old Westbury, NY: Feminist Press, 1983. Ellen Carol DuBois, *Feminism and Suffrage: The Emergence of an Independent Women's Movement in America, 1848-1869*, (DuBois) Ithaca, Cornell University Press, 1978 and Nancy A. Hewitt, *Women's Activism and Social Change, Rochester, New York, 1822-1872, (Hewitt)* Ithaca, Cornell University Press, 1984.

45. Estrelda Y. Alexander, *Women of Azusa Street* (Cleveland: Pilgrim Press, 2005), 12.

46. Ibid., 37-38.

47. Cheryl Sanders, *Saints in Exile* (New York: Oxford University Press, 1996), 16.

48. Acts 2:17.

49. Luke 4: 18.

50. Paul Tillich, *Theology and Culture* (New York: Oxford Press, 1959), 42.

51. Langdon Gilkey, "The Spirit and the Discovery of Truth through Dialogue" in *Experience of the Spirit* (New York: Seabury Press, 1974), 60-61.

44. By Localized cultural hermeneutic, I mean that biblical hermeneutics must be sensitive to the culture within which the gospel is proclaimed.

52. Margaret M. Poloma, "The Pentecostal Movement." Available from http://hirr.hartsem.edu/research/pentecostalism_polomaart5.html (accessed 15 January 2008), 9.

53. Rodney Stark, "A Taxonomy of Religious Experience", *Journal for the Scientific Study of Religion* (5) (1965), 99. This taxonomy is also quoted in Poloma's "The Pentecostal Movement," 9.

54. For the question of relativity, see Gilkey, 61.

55. Ibid.

56. Ibid.

57. Shane Clifton, "The Spirit and Doctrinal Development: A Functional Analysis of the Traditional Pentecostal Doctrine of the Baptism in the Holy Spirit" *Pneuma* 29, 1 (2007), 16.

58. Scriptural references that refer to "Spirit Baptism" or "baptism of the Holy Spirit" include Luke 3:16; Matt 3:11; John 1:33b; Acts 1:5; Acts 11:16 and I Cor 12:13.

59. Amos Yong, *Discerning the Spirit(s): A Pentecostal-Charismatic Contribution to Christian Theology of Religions* (Sheffield, England: Sheffield Academic Press Ltd, 2000), 17.

60. Examples of how traditionally acclaimed Pentecostal-type churches use Scripture to interpret forthcoming experiences include centuries-old debates over apocalypticism and millennialism. Pentecostal-type churches remain in intense debates over these issues.

61. The Rock of Life Church would more closely align with neo-Pentecostalism than would A Church of God, Pillar of the Truth. The Rock of Life Church does not subscribe to the doctrine of "initial evidence." The "initial evidence" argument is that all "Spirit-filled Christians must speak in tongues.

62. Yong, 17. Also, see, Harvey Cox, *Fire From Heaven: The Rise of Pentecostal Spirituality and the Reshaping of Religion in The Twenty-first Century* (Reading, MA: Addison-Wesley Publishing Company, 1995).

Chapter 5

A Proposal: The Trilateral Paradigm in the Life of the Church

The first chapter explains the faulty theological premises of several doctrinal practices in pentecostal-type churches. The congregations in Chapter two illustrate the ramifications of these premises, as expressed in weak biblical interpretations for doctrinal practices often oppressive, mainly to women. Chapters three and four suggest a process for correcting the problems of theological processes at the root of many of the biblically unsound practices among independent pentecostal churches. These last two chapters involved a systematic theological examination and appliance of a proposed trilateral hermeneutic—Scripture, experiences of the Holy Spirit, and culture.

A major issue among independent pentecostal churches is their ecclesial structure. An enormous amount of ecclesial power rests in the hands of the senior leader (e.g. bishop or pastor). The trilateral works best as shared-praxis within community rather than by unilateral adjudication. In this final chapter, I propose a strategy (*a la* Browning)[1] of shared-praxis for incorporating the trilateral in ecclesial structures of independent pentecostal churches. This effort follows Browning's fourth movement of practical theology and relies heavily on Groome's work in Christian education.[2]

Many independent pentecostal churches need a leadership model and communal formation with an educational paradigm rooted in the trilateral for rigorous analysis of doctrinal practices. Many of them have ecclesial paradigms with leadership structures that subscribe to theological methods, which render oppressive church practices antithetical to the liberating nature of the Spirit and the community of faith model of church. There needs to be a renewal of pentecostal-type ethos within the ecclesiology of these churches. The ethos must be cultivated by the liberating nature of the Spirit to foster stronger communal synergy that includes the whole congregation.

Among some of the churches (particularly those of the African descent), there is often little distinction between theology, biblical interpretation and Christian education. These categories seem to overlap. Therefore, as I have set theology and biblical interpretation in dialogue in the former chapters, I would like to bring Christian education into the conversation of practical theological renewal. Christian education might inform a reimaged practical theology for these churches within the churches might strengthen their ecclesial theological structures. As a result, the doctrine would be more viable towards achieving the mission of the gospel and what Paul imagines it means for Christians to be "in Christ."

By way of practical application, the churches might offer an annual educational forum (similar to annual business meetings) dedicated to a rigorous systematic analysis of doctrinal practices, based on a critical usage of the trilateral (as treated in the former chapters). This forum should include diversified (gender, age, role of leadership and lay people) representatives for shared reflection on church theology and doctrinal practice. The representatives will gather around a theological framework. I have proffered the trilateral. A suggested model for the meeting might be something like a Quaker meeting in that everyone present should be given liberty to speak. The God of the community will speak through everyone. This will disempowered the increasing unilateral theological, doctrinal, and spiritual control granted to one person, the bishop or pastor. The bishop or pastor would serve as facilitator and guide. But everyone would share freely at a roundtable-type forum (*a la* Letty Russell).

Both the Rock of Life Church and the Church of God, Pillar of the Truth Church exemplify the need for a critical theological strategy to reshape doctrinal practices. Their current theological methods seem at times uncritical and other times plainly incoherent. The result is oppressive practices, antithetical to the nature of the gospel and contradictory to their own claims on the liberating Spirit. These churches maintain theological autonomy as they are unattached to denominational hierarchy and restraints. My concern, however, is that theological autonomy entrusted in one (often uncritically trained) person (usually a male) often leads to equally uncritical doctrinal practices, as seems to be the case at the Rock of Life Church and the Church of God, Pillar of the Truth.

In *Pentecostal Formation: Pedagogy among the Oppressed* Cheryl Bridges John applauds the classical pentecostal churches for their ethos of the Spirit within which the community of faith is formed.[3] However, as we embrace the twenty-first century, there is a greater emergence of independent pentecostal churches. Most independent African American pentecostal churches maintain theological autonomy as they are unattached to denominational hierarchy and restraints.

Some church leaders of African Descent in the twentieth century such as Father Major Jealous Divine, original name George Baker, founder of the Peace Mission, and Bishop C.M. Grace, known to his followers as Sweet Sweet Daddy Grace, founder and leader of the United House of Prayer for All People, started their communities of faith as charismatic leaders who expressed love and concern for people --- mainly poor people.[4] They won their followers' trust such that many of their followers forsook their own families to follow these alleged "men of God." Followers blindly trusted these men in the areas of finance, politics, and theology. As strange as many of their doctrinal practices seem to us today, the Christian education in these churches did not allow for critical shared-praxis. If it did, the members could have step back and, along with the leadership, critically reflected on those practices. They could have boldly raised awareness to the strange teachings. The communities might have escaped the long-lasting oppression that their leaders inflicted. And a new ecclesial direction might have been determined for the church communities affiliated with the fellowships.

Unlike these particular communities, some other twentieth century movements that mirror the type of unilateral church leadership advanced at the Peace Movement and The United House of Prayer for All People led their followers to oppressive practices and, in these extreme cases, their premature graves. These church leaders were of European Descent and included David Koresh of the "Branch Davidians" in Waco, Texas, in the 1990s, Jim (James) Jones of the "People's Temple" and "Jonestown" in Guyana, in the 1970s, and Marshall Applewhite of "Heaven's Gate" in Rancho Santa Fe, California, in the 1990s.[5]

Evidence renders that unilateral leadership risks the lack of insight into the multiple locations of people within the community and theologically dangerous because it places an enormous amount of power in the hands of a single person. The danger is amplified when such communities lack structures of accountability and communal forums for critical reflection. Independent pentecostal churches need ecclesiological structures that safeguard them from theologies arbitrarily imposed by leaders who may possess certain gifts, but lack adequate tools for theological praxis. I contend, moreover, that the burden or privilege of determining church doctrine and polity should not rest in the hands of the senior pastor (usually a male) alone. The independent pentecostal churches would benefit greatly from a robust strategy extended to the entire congregation that empowers the entire community of God's people to participate constructively in theological matters.

Dependence upon Pastoral Leadership

Pastors are key (even sometimes dominate) figures in independent African American pentecostal churches. There was a well-known independent pentecostal bishop/senior pastor from Atlanta, GA, preaching in a conference in Raleigh, N.C. While sitting on the auditorium's stage with the other bishops and pastors, I observed how intently the attendees listened to him. However, I was stunned at the weakness of content in the pastor's sermon. He commented in the sermon that "God is asleep and it's our duty to wake God up." I have also heard this pastor preach sermons full of comments that I disagree with theologically. Recently, in conversation with a friend, I mentioned my dissent to this pastor's preaching. At first, she wanted to avoid the conversation. Then, she asserted, "Don't put your mouth on the man of God!" Now, I think this pastor might be a good man. He is doing good things for the community there in Atlanta. However, he said something about God that violates my understanding of God. And frankly, one wonders if his comment about God being asleep set well with more than half of the people in that auditorium. Yet, because many pentecostal-type congregants are conditioned to accept what the pastor or bishop says as truth regardless of how ridiculous it might seem, they tend to remain silent on the issue. My friend's comment to me finds commonplace among African American pentecostal-type churches.

Widely, pastors are revered similarly to God's chief agent of instruction for the everyday life of believers. So, even if people choose not to comply, they are not willing to engage a conversation of critique. In this sense, the pastoral role extends beyond proclaiming the gospel; it includes theological authority, eschatological insight, life coaching, agency of healing, financial counseling, and more.

In this constituency, parishioners believe that their faith, success, and eternal destiny are closely tied to their reverence for the pastoral position. For example, when parishioners are sick, many call the pastor before they call 911. Alternatively, when parishioners are considering a major purchase (e.g., a house or car), they ask God in prayer but seek the wisdom of the pastor, hoping to hear confirmation that the purchase is the will of God. Parishioners rely on the pastor to teach them God's will for living a life pleasing to the Lord. Many sacrifice their own insight for the mind of God allegedly revealed through the pastor. Simply stated, in independent pentecostal churches, the pastor has great power -- often a rather unilateral muscle of control.

Pastors are designated, "chief priest" or "angel of the house." It is taboo to refer to these "chief priests" or "angels of the house," by their birth name only. One must address them as "pastor," "reverend," "brother," "apostle," or "bishop." "Pastor as teacher" is a designation highly esteemed at many of the churches. The pastor's very words are treasured as gold, even if they are not critically rational or theologically sound. Consequently, the pastor's theological reflections are seldom openly challenged and if they are, the interlocutor is silenced. To challenge the pastor is to risk exclusion in many pentecostal-type churches. Obviously, challenging the pastor does not have the same level of prohibition in all churches. Yet, at some level most of these churches maintain a high reverence for the theological authority of the pastor as teacher.

By maintaining "theological authority of the pastor as teacher," some of these churches adhere to what Seymour and Miller call "reclaiming the dialectic between theology and teaching that has been reflected through the history of the church." They call for the role of pastor as primary theologian for the community.[6] However, in churches where the pastor has not been adequately trained, his or her doctrinal teachings may inhibit the theological growth of the community. In some cases, individuals sacrifice their own rational thinking, cultural identity and even their sense of call (as in women sensing the call to ordained ministry) on the altar of oppression to adhere uncritically to doctrinal practices seldom discerned through shared-praxis.

The Rev. B. Courtney McBath, senior pastor and bishop of Calvary Revival Church in Norfolk, Virginia notes this problem. He tells the story of a church community that went on a skating trip; a young lady was standing on the sideline of the skating center, choosing not to skate. Urging the young lady to join in with the fun, the pastor said to her, "You should out there and skate." Without questioning or offering descent, the young lady got skates and started skating.

She skated until she was dog-tired. Palpitating, sweating and dizzy, the young lady skated over to the pastor as said, "Can I please stop skating now?"

The point here is that this woman revered her ministers so highly that she sacrificed her choice not to skate to adhere to the pastor's recommendation to skate. McBath explains that in some pentecostal-type circles, the pastor's voice is exchanged for the voice of God. In the illustration, the young woman did not even want to stop skating until her pastor gave permission. The sentiments of this story are typical in many of pentecostal-type circles.

Christians within these circles are often comfortable to lift a human leader to God's proxy. Such Christians must rediscover their own experience of the Holy Spirit as viable contribution to their own life as well as the life of the Church. Spiritual experience of the pastor and the voice of the pastor must de-center the church. Otherwise, the pastor risks becoming the object of idol worship and the congregation fails to know its voice in divine matters.

Perhaps, the high consideration for pastoral leadership, particularly, among African American churches reaches as far back as slavery. Preachers such as Richard Allen, Benjamin Chew, Nat Turner, William Lloyd Garrison, Sojourner Truth (Isabella Baumfree), John Jasper were often leaders in abolition of slavery and in comforting the slaves during severe turmoil on the plantations. They often were the spiritual, theological and social champions that helped their slave congregations to deal with the mayhem of the day.

Jumping forward to the Civil Rights movement, one might recognize that projects historically effective in African American communities began in what Robert Franklin call the "anchor institutions."[7] The anchor institutions are the "family," schools," and "churches." For the purposes of this chapter, I focus only one of these "anchor institutions," and that is the churches. The church was and remains the Town hall of the African American communities. In the most recent election, President Barack Obama spent a lot of time in conversation with pastors, particularly African American pastors. He even shared sermons from the African American pulpit several times during the course of his campaign for president. Obama knows that the primary way to get to the African American community, even now, is through the church. The church remains the Town hall of the Black communities. The African American classical pentecostal denomination--the Church of God in Christ—was one of those anchor institutions in the African American community during the Civil Rights movement.

David Daniels, an African American pentecostal church historian, notes that, since the Civil Rights Movement, African American pentecostalism has contributed to the religious landscape of America in that it has produced political activists and provided platforms for political activists to express the concerns of African American people.[8] These activists were mainly church leaders who saw their role in the community as social servants. They led the churches in efforts to reform the socio-political structures of the American society. With the oppressed in mind, they had a larger vision for a reformed society in sight. They sought to educate the oppressed in critical social critique but also self conscious reflection. These church leaders employed the workings of the Holy Spirit in empowering the poor and disenfranchised people, socially. These leaders were advocates for the interests of the people and not themselves. Their teachings were directly connected to the liberating power of the Holy Spirit to reform people and justice systems for all people. An example is the headquarters for the Church of God in Christ – Mason Temple Church of God in Christ – which served as a focal point of civil rights activities in Memphis during the 1950s and 1960s.

The emerging non-classical and non-denominational pentecostal churches (the churches that I have called independent pentecostal churches) have similar centrality of the Spirit as the classical pentecostal churches. I believe that these churches have similar potential to perpetuate the workings of the Holy Spirit in shaping communities and in empowering the furtherance of theological reformation in oppressive, irresponsible church doctrine. However, if independent African American pentecostal churches are to re-image theologically, they need a new ecclesial paradigm, less pastor-centered and less unilaterally steered.

One wonders if the unilateral church leadership of churches competes with the workings of the Holy Spirit. Perhaps the churches need a communal strategy for producing church doctrine that reflects the liberating work of the Holy Spirit. A proposal in Christian education that invites the liberating nature of the Holy Spirit would sustain both the social and theological dynamics essential to the viability of independent churches.

Christian Education as Strategy

I recommend Thomas Groome's community-focused Christian educational paradigm as strategy for revitalizing the social consciousness as well as stimulating a communal theological model for reshaped doctrinal practices. Groome's educational method stresses the need for *participation, partnership* and *dialogue* and requires a discursive communal process. I agree with Browning's assertion that the structure of theological praxis and the dynamics of Christian education should be the same; both should entail the same procedures.[9] I propose, moreover, that Pastoral and congregational leadership in the independent churches should engage a methodology of "shared praxis," a thoughtful and continuous process for addressing theology and practice. "Shared praxis" in Christian education involves the entire community of faith and seems to be a viable path for these churches in social and theological matters. Groome's Christian education methods of *participation, partnership and dialogue,* furthermore, might guide these churches into a communal (shared) praxis around the trilateral.

As ecclesial entities with no denominational hierarchy, independent churches are in an excellent position to formalize a Christian education model that begins with the concerns of the congregation. Congregations and leaders should filter those concerns through experiences of the Holy Spirit, readings of Scripture and perceptions of culture (what this book refers to as the *trilateral*), re-examining doctrinal practices by critically examining theological tenets central to Spirit-filled editions of Christianity.

Moreover, I recommend Groome's Christian education model of "shared praxis," rather than the model advanced by Seymour and Miller in "Openings to

God: Education and Theology in Dialogue" mentioned above. The "shared" communal dynamics of Christian education seem lacking in Seymour and Miller. The top-down paternalistic paradigm that reflects dominant western religious paternalism that for centuries has shaped the mainstream religious landscape in America.

Problem: Historical Top-down Paternalism Engrained in Western Christianity

In the nineteenth century, two missiologists, Rufus Anderson and Henry Venn, condemned the western paternalistic model for Christian missions. In Warren B. Newberry's "Contextualizing Indigenous Church Principles: an African Model" he points out that "both Venn and Anderson formulated their principles in a crisis situation reacting to the extreme paternalism propagated and enjoyed by their western counterparts. They were opposed to the making of 'rice Christians,' an approach that caused total dependence on the sending mission to sustain the work and employ the believing nationals."[10] In the twentieth century, missiologists such as Melvin Hodges and Roland Allen[11] sought to sustain the grassroots indigenous formation of churches and to include ordinary Christians in processes of Church leadership.

Relating the discussion of missions to the current discussion of theological judgment and leadership in the independent pentecostal churches of today, the paternalistic model in ecclesiological structures of these churches is reminiscent of the old problem in western religious leadership. The paternalistic model present in these churches esteems the pastor higher in theological access than the ordinary Christian in the pews. Such pattern sets the stage for the exclusion of multiple voices from theological discourse when determining church doctrine. A "shared" communal praxis model may help these churches break open the otherwise closed hermeneutical processes for re-examining doctrine and reshaping doctrinal practices sensitive to the often oppressed ones in the church.

Core Principles at Risk

I believe that the top-down ministry paradigm commonplace among independent pentecostal churches risk at least two very important values to the call of the Christian church. First of all, the working of the pneumato-Christological union that centers the ecclesial identity of pentecostal-type churches is in compromise. The working of the Holy Spirit (pneumatokos) is central to the body of Christ notion in the pentecostal-type churches. A key biblical teaching in the gospel where the Spirit and Christ are united is Luke 4:18-19. When the Spirit comes upon Christ in Luke 4:18-19 it anoints Christ to preach and implement social consciousness on behalf of the oppressed: "The Spirit of the Lord is upon me because She has anointed Me to preach the gospel to the poor' She has sent Me to heal the brokenhearted, to proclaim liberty to the captives and recovery of sight to the blind, to set at liberty those who are oppressed; to proclaim the year of freedom."

Secondly, the Great Commission is in compromise: "Go... baptizing them in the name of the Father and of the Son and of the Holy Spirit..." Most pentecostal-type churches have always made immersion their only method of baptism. The giving up of self and putting on divine identity is at least by in large central to most theologies of baptism in these churches. In Matthew 28:19, Christ charges His emissaries to baptize or immerse people from everywhere in the same identity of the Godhead. This means that all people are granted access to the "deep things of God."

However, many independent pentecostal churches revere the pastor for an assumed special access to the "deep things of God." Such assumption elevates the pastor's theological judgment and honors it as voice of God. Communal participation or discernment from the congregation is not commonplace among this growing constituency of independent pentecostal churches. The congregants, then, become people immersed in the identity of an individual (Pastor Such and Such's church), which is contrary to the Great Commission which charges ministers to immerse people in the identity of the Godhead. The Great Commission implies that common people of the church of Christ are invited to share equal access to the knowledge of God and not just the unilateral voice of a the minister. If the church is to reflect the theology of baptism that invites all to an immersion in the knowledge of God, it becomes important that all of Christ's disciples (expressed in congregations) share in communal praxis for the formation of theology for church doctrinal practice.

Pastor as Practical Theological Guide: Getting Back On Track

I propose a model of "pastor as practical theological guide." In this model, the pastor is no longer the sole agent of truth or final determinant of doctrinal practices; neither is the pastoral role relegated to an egalitarian presence within the congregation. The latter role might deny the spiritual authority of the pastor or accord too much authority to the assembly. In the "pastor as practical theological guide" model, the pastor facilitates practical strategies for Christian education in the community's call for a trilateral process for doctrinal practices.

Farley's logic is helpful in defining my proposition of "pastor as theological guide." In *Theologia: The Fragmentation and Unity of Theological Education,* Farley proposes a model of Christian education that is *theologia-centered*; it parallels the Greco-Roman educational model called *paideia*. Farley explains that *paideia* is the educational process of culturing human beings *toward* virtue.[12] *Theologia* is, moreover, "the ecclesial counterpart to *paideia*."[13] I understand Farley's concept of *theologia* to mean – in a process of God-related decision-making – the culturing of the congregation *toward* "sapiential knowledge engendered by grace and divine self-disclosure."[14] Applied to the model of "pastor as practical theological guide," *theologia* means that the pastor becomes responsible for facilitating critical tools (the trilateral) for the church membership and leadership. These tools would include critical theological skills, such as biblical criticism and exegesis that the pastor has developed through formal training. These tools would also include exploratory skills for theological reflection on the activity of the Holy Spirit and the dynamics of culture.

To implement appropriately the "pastor as practical theological guide" model, it is crucial that pastors of independent pentecostal churches receive formal theological education. In order to establish viable a Christian education program, the pastor needs adequate tools in the areas of biblical studies, pentecostal spirituality, and cultural anthropology. The trilateral is highlighted as an integral discipline in critical formation of theological tenets and doctrinal practices central to independent pentecostal churches. Therefore, study in these areas would help to sharpen the mind of the pastor for culturing the congregation *toward* shared ecclesial praxis. The goal is divine revelation in doctrinal practices pertaining to concrete situations or issues. The pastor, as theological guide, acknowledges that divine revelation can emerge from a communal discernment process, and is not limited to a unilateral determination of the "pastor as teacher" model.

A church that periodically revisits its theology to reconsider doctrine is a church led by a person with a self-reflection similar to Paul's self-reflection when he wrote the following: "Not that I have already obtained this or am already perfect; but I press on to make it my own, because Christ Jesus has made me his own. Beloved, I do not consider that I have made it my own; but this one thing I do: forgetting what lies behind and straining forward to what lies ahead, I press toward the goal for the prize of the heavenly call of God in Christ Jesus."[15] However, if this issue of incoherent theological criteria and unilateral theological authority persists, future possibilities for pentecostal-type churches "press" toward a negative end and not toward the heavenly call of God in Christ Jesus (ref. Phil 3:14).

Independent pentecostal churches should include within their ecclesial structure and on their church calendars workshops for theological reflection on congregational issues/doctrinal practices. These workshops would offer a context for shared-praxis in employing communal insight on theological matters. Just as in annual church business meetings, when the entire faith community assembles to discuss forthcoming business for the next year, they might set aside time for the congregation to raise theological concerns over church doctrine and practices.

Koinonia

Koinonia is a Greek term often used in Scripture as major character of the early church. Acts 2:42 describes the earliest church as one that continued daily in apostolic teachings and *koinonia*. Koinonia is often translated as "fellowship." However, there are several other words that are appropriate to the translation of the Greek word koinonia, terms such as "partnership," sharing," "participation," "social intercourse," and "communication."[16] These terms expand the concept of koinonia beyond our socialized understanding of "fellowship." Thus, the Acts 2:42 passage suggests that while the apostles were slated teachers, the congregation had a role in the teaching-learning process, a role beyond being good listeners. Rather, the congregation participated in the teaching process as they engaged each other in sharing their thoughts and experiences of the Holy Spirit. Throughout the earliest church, particularly in Acts, the sharing of experiences of the Holy Spirit and the continued discourse among believers concerning the relationship between Hebrew thought, Greco-Roman thought and the new found faith in Jesus helped to shape the earliest church.

Often, in the churches today, koinonia is relegated to a shared dinner in the church's kitchen, a church member's house, or in what some churches call "the fellowship hall." In both cases, fellowship focuses a time and place to eat chicken, collard greens and to drink ice tea, mostly, after a Sunday morning, a Saturday Sabbath service or church conference. There is a need for a broader understanding of koinonia that might assist churches in more inclusive participation in theological understandings for doctrine more faithful to the gospel of Jesus Christ.

While koinonia might include table fellowship, it is deeper than merely a time for eating. The concept of biblical koinonia is a time for building partnerships for common purpose and permitting another to share. Koinonia speaks to the sharing of ideas and experiences as part of the formation churches need for stronger doctrine. Instead, as at COGPOTC and ROLC, described in chapter two, independent pentecostal churches often short circuit koinonia. The church leadership often seems to fear that inviting the congregation into shared-praxis might threaten unilateral male dominated doctrinal decisions and thereby violate the common bond of doctrine imposed upon the congregation. However, I believe that a more expansive insight into biblical Koinonia provides another forum within the church for healthy theological discourse and not simply biblical justification for a fellowship hall to exchange our best and most favorable dishes. Koinonia is a viable biblical notion wherein members for the congregation gather and dialogue over issues, using something like my proposed trilateral as framework for theological discussions for relevant conclusions more faithful to the liberating gospel.

Independent pentecostal churches might benefit from this broader understanding of koinonia, incorporating it as part of a praxis-oriented Christian education. The churches' theological health would increase in this notion of koinonia as they share experiences of the Holy Spirit, readings of scripture, and perceptions of culture (the trilateral). Pastors should be willing to not only speak as the Spirit gives utterance, but also to hear what the Spirit is saying to and through the congregations. This process would increase the potential for exposing doctrinal practices as oppressive and antithetical to the Christian faith. Broadly speaking of the independent pentecostal church, the partnership model would help minimize the development of probable church cults as more "partnership" churches are planted daily.

Groome: Partnership, Participation, and Dialogue

Partnership

In the spirit of koinonia, Thomas Groome offers a practical Christian education program within the area of "shared praxis" which might serve as model in theological discourse for doctrine that involves members of the congregation. Groome's paradigm is three-pronged:"partnership, participation and dialogue"[17] could be a possible guide towards a leadership paradigm. By "partnership," Groome transcends the traditional top-down approach, whereby the teacher delivers knowledge and the students receive it.[18] The "partnership" dynamic demands a conversation between teacher and students. This interactive dynamic calls the teacher to a new self-image, away from "the answer person" or controller of knowledge, toward "being with" participants in a subject-to-subject relationship.[19] Groome further explains that this "partnership" model does not forgo the teachers' role as "enablers and resource persons."[20] Rather, it removes the unilateral leadership model. I suggest replacing the top-down, unilateral model with a circular model. In the circular paradigm, the pastor is willing "to learn as well as to teach, to listen as well as to talk, to be questioned as well as to question, and to use one's training and resources to empower rather than to control the teaching/learning partnership."[21]

Letty Russell offers a round table approach to theology in *Church in the Round*. The roundtable approach is Russell's visual for doing theology that invites voices from the margins to theological table, where their voices can be heard in theological discourse. Her rationale is that God invites everyone to the discovery of God's divine self-disclosure. Russell's roundtable approach is sustained by Groome's "partnership" model. Her roundtable approach acknowledges the Christians role in the educational process. It welcomes ongoing communal interactions with religious leaders as facilitators of the ongoing process towards a more critical discovery of divine self-disclosure.[22]

In accord with Russell and Groome, the pastor should not bear full theological responsibility, blame, or credit, for doctrinal practices. The community, as the circle of faith, must move forward into deeper insights of God's will for doctrinal, as well as church ministry, practices. The circle of the roundtable never ends. Such an evolutionary process is captured in Segundo's "hermeneutical circle." The hermeneutical circle entails the pastor's willingness to reinterpret theology for possible revisions in theological practice. The hermeneutical circle, moreover, is like an upward spiral, propelling the faith community toward more critical and relevant insights for determining church practices.

In the hermeneutical circle, both teacher and student participate as partners and the entire community benefits. Groome adds, "True partnership demands a kind of ongoing conversion of all participants."[23] Therefore, Christian education based on this partnership is not a model that simply imparts theological knowledge or imposes doctrinal practices from the pastor's office alone. Rather, the partnership model extends Christian education into theological discernment and governance of the church.

Participation

Groome's "shared praxis" model exemplifies pedagogy that invites the participation of the membership to gain insight from the range of people involved in the educational process. No member of the church would be excluded. The participatory nature of the process dictates that everyone be a student of theology while everyone is, to a degree, a potential theological agent. All members, therefore, should be invited to express, reflect, encounter, appropriate and contribute to reshaping doctrinal practices.[24]

Traditionally, independent pentecostal churches demand that the membership remain in compliance with accepted doctrinal practices. While particular doctrinal practices may diverge dramatically between independent pentecostal churches, compliance within the local church is often required for membership. And since strident compliance is so characteristic for these churches, I believe the lay membership along with the pastoral leadership should participate in the practical theological enterprise for shaping and reshaping doctrinal practices.

Dialogue

The unilateral authority of theological leadership in many of these churches creates a privileged class system within the body of Christ. Only the pastors are granted the authority to discern truth to deliver to the congregation in the form of doctrinal practices. Groome says that such a paradigm is inconsistent with Paul's claim that "every Christian is a member of the Body of Christ, and no one is less a member of it than any other Christian."[25] Groome adds that Paul's statements on ethnic, social and gender equality (I Cor. 12:13 and Gal. 3:28) "should be at the foundation of Christian communities now, and how they educate must be radically communal."[26]

To this end, Groome's work encourages communal dialogue in Christian education and ecclesial formation. Building on Groome's concept of dialogue, I propose that the churches build a Christian education system, structured by the communal dynamics of the shared praxis approach, to foster dialogue and conversation. This conversation is not simply between two or more people; rather, the conversation is both internal and communal. Whether the conversation is individual or communal, God is at the center of the dialogue. Therefore, the dialogue should include prayer and meditation that seeks the guidance of the Holy Spirit. Through the Holy Spirit, God speaks to and through all who engage the dialogue.

Conclusion

This project offers a corrective process for theological problems observed at two independent pentecostal churches of the African Diaspora, including, but not limited to, observations of the Rock of Life Church and A Church of God, Pillar of the Truth. The trilateral paradigm is comprised of interpretations of Scripture, experiences of the Holy Spirit, and perceptions of culture. All of the Spirit-filled members of the members of the congregations have access to the trilateral. Therefore, doctrinal judgment should not be the discretion of the senior pastor unilaterally. Groome's shared-praxis model provides practical example of how a congregational model theological forum might look.

I have explained that when the trilateral is strategically administered, it diminishes oppressive doctrine uncritically imposed theological doctrine is exposed. This will support the church's encounter with culture in isolating oppressive practices. Through the illustrations, I have exposed two oppressive doctrinal practices, one related to culture, the other related to gender.

As stated in chapter three, I recognize that some scholars might believe that the example of "women wearing trousers or pants" is not worth mentioning in a scholarly book. Some may conclude that the superficiality of the issue reduces the cultural argument to less than sufficient. Yet, in my observation superficial attire issues remain real and generate much contention among pentecostal-type Christians and the doctrine of congregations to whom these Christians belong even to the extent of splintering congregations and creating divisions among church fellowships globally. Superficial issues, along with other more complex issues, affect evangelism, church growth, and ecumenism. However, it is difficult to engage more complex issues such as abortion, polygamy, climate-change, same-sex marriage, divorce and re-marriage when the issues that seem simple dominate the life of the congregation. Without more critical theological structures for responding to these issues, the superficial will continue to dominate discussions and other issues as mentioned will remain undertreated

Moreover, I contend that the issue of "holy attire," as superficial as it sometimes seems, represents the kind of practices that emerge from a deeply rooted theological plague that results from unresolved considerations for the role of culture in biblical hermeneutics. The issue of "holy attire" seems often exemplary of the illogical doctrinal practices that emerge from an underdeveloped practical theological enterprise within pentecostal-type churches. Such underdeveloped theological activity has dominated the making of church doctrine and polity for more than a century. The aim of this book has been to create strategies for a new theological paradigm. This book has sought to expose this important problem and offers strategies to remedy it. I hope my treatment might assist these churches in reformulating more critical practices for the future of independent pentecostal churches.

In short, theological problems of biblical interpretation have caused ecclesial problems. I have suggested that a trilateral has positive ramifications for resolving ecclesial problems. In this final chapter, I have proposed a "strategic practical theology" for a shared praxis model of Christian education for independent pentecostal churches such as the Rock of Life Church and the Church of God, Pillar of the Truth. I have argued that pastors need formal theological training for the role of "pastor as theological guide." I have also argued that shared-praxis reduces the detrimental power of unilateral church-leadership and curves the likelihood of generating oppressive doctrinal practices. The partnership, participation, and dialogical process, as Groome proffers, includes the voices of the congregation in the theological enterprise *toward* reshaping ecclesial praxis in the love and liberation of the gospel.

Notes

1. By "strategic proposal," I am using Browning's language of the fourth movement in what he calls a "fundamental practical theology." See section on "a strategic proposal" or "a fully practical theology" in Don S. Browning, *A Fundamental Practical Theology* (Minneapolis: Fortress Press, 1991). The "strategic proposal" is the final movement, which outlines recommendations for a revised practice.

2. Thomas Groome, "Theology on Our Feet: A Revisionist Pedagogy for Healing the Gap between Academia and Ecclesia," *Formation and Reflection*, Lewis Mudge and James Poling (eds.), 55-78 (Philadelphia: Fortress Press, 1987), 57. Browning refers to Groome's position on a practical theological approach to Christian education in *A Fundamental Practical Theology* (Minneapolis: Fortress Press, 1991), 218.

3. Cheryl Bridges Johns, *Pentecostal Formation: A Pedagogy among the Oppressed.* (Sheffield: Sheffield Academic Press, 1993) 8.

4. See, http://www.pbs.org/thisfarbyfaith/journey_3/p_10.html (accessed 28. October 2008) and http://www.britannica.com/EBchecked/topic/166561/Father-Divine (accessed 28 October 2008). Also see http://capeverde-islands.com/grace.html (accessed 28 October 2008) and http://archive.southcoasttoday.com/daily/10-96/10-21-96/b01li035.htm (accessed 28 October 2008). Though they the communal practices highly revere their unilateral leaders and bare cultic remnants, their leadership is not reported to have led masses of their people to commit suicide.

5. This list of unilateral-type leaders is all white leaders who led their followers to their premature death. I have included them because their leadership style is consistent with that of many African American church leaders. Their demise might serve as example of the destiny of others who subscribe to the unilateral leadership that mirrors these men.

6. Jack L. Seymour and Donald E. Miller, "Openings to God: Education and Theology in Dialogue," in *Theological Approaches to Christian Education*, Jack L. Seymour and Donald E. Miller (eds) (Nashville: Abingdon Press, 1990), 23.

7. Robert M. Franklin, *Crisis in the Village: Restoring Hope in African American Communities (*Minneapolis: Fortress Press, 2007), 3.

8. David D. Daniels III, "'Doing All the Good We Can': The Political Witness of African American Holiness and Pentecostal Churches in the Post-Civil Rights Era," in *New Day Begun: African American Churches and Civic Culture in Post-Civil Rights America*, R. Drew Smith (ed.), (Durham: Duke University Press, 2003), 164.

9. Don S. Browning, *A Fundamental Practical Theology* (Minneapolis: Fortress Press, 1991), 218.

10. Warren B. Newberry, "Contextualizing Indigenous Church Principles: an African Model," in *Asian Journal of Pentecostal Studies* 8:1 (2005), 106.

11. To read more on Hodges' mission theory, see Melvin L. Hodges, *The indigenous Church* (Springfield: Gospel Publishing House), 1953. To read more on Allen's mission theory, see Roland Allen, *Missionary Methods: St. Paul's or Ours?* (Grand Rapids: Wm. B. Eerdmans Publishing Company, 1962).

12. Edward Farley, *Theologia: The Fragmentation and Unity of Theological Education* (Philadelphia: Fortress Press, 1983), 152-153.
13. Ibid., 153.
14. Ibid.
15. Philippians 3:12-14.
16. See, F. Wilbur Gingrich, and Frederick W. Danker. *A Greek-English Lexicon of New Testament and Other Early Christian Literature.* (Chicago: University of Chicago Press, 1979), 438-439. Also see, James, A Strong. *Concise Dictionary of the Words in the Greek Testament: With their Renderings in the Authorized English Version.* (Nashville: Thomas Nelson Publishers, 1990), 42
17. Thomas H. Groome, *Sharing Faith: A Comprehensive Approach to Religious Education and Pastoral Ministry – The Way for Shared Praxis* (New York: HarperCollins Publishers, 1991), 143.
18. Ibid.
19. Ibid.
20. Ibid.
21. Ibid.
22. Letty M. Russell, *Church in the Round: Feminist Interpretation of the Church* (Louisville, Kentucky: Westminster/John Knox Press, 1993). The theme of partnership in Groome is supported in Russell as he admits to have been influenced by her works (see notes in Groome, *Sharing Faith*, 485); Letty M. Russell, *Christian Education in Mission* (Philadelphia: Westminster Press, 1967), *The Future of Partnership* (Philadelphia: Westminster Press, 1979), and *Growth in Partnership* (Philadelphia: Westminster Press, 1981).
23. Groome, *Sharing Faith*, 143.
24. Groome, *Sharing Faith*, 144.
25. Ibid., 142.
26. Ibid., 142-143.

Bibliography

Abraham, K.C. *Liberative Solidarity: Contemporary Perspectives on Mission.* Christava Sahitya Samithi, Tiruvalle, 1996.
Abraham, William. *The Logic of Evangelism.* Grand Rapids: William B. Eerdmans Publishing Co., 1989.
Abrams, Minnie F. *The Baptism of the Holy Ghost and Fire.* 2nd ed. Kedgaon, India: Mukti Mission Press, 1906.
Adogame, Afe, Gerloff. Roswith. Hock, Klaus, *The Shaping of Christianity in Africa and the African Diaspora.* London: Continuum, 2008.
Allen, Roland. *Missionary Methods; St. Paul's or Ours?* Grand Rapids: William B. Eerdmans Publishing Co.,1962.
Allen, Roland. *The Ministry of the Spirit.* Grand Rapids: William B. Eerdmans Publishing Co., 1962
Anderson, Allan. *An Introduction to Pentecostalism: Global Charismatic Christianity.* United Kingdom: University of Cambridge, 2004.
_____. "Challenges and Prospects for Research into AICs in Southern Africa," Paper read at the Centre for the Study of Christianity in the Non-Western World, University of Edinburgh, January 1996, *Missionalia* 23:3, November 1995. 283-294.
_____."The Gospel and Culture in Pentecostal Mission in the Third World." Paper presented at the 9th Conference of the European Pentecostal Charismatic Research Association, Missions Academy, University of Hamburg, Germany, (July 1999). http://www.epcra.ch/papers_pdf/hamburg/anderson_1999.pdf (accessed 21 December 2007).
_____. *Zion and Pentecost: The Spirituality and Experience of Pentecostal and Three Zionist/Apostolic Churches in South Africa.* Africa Initiatives in Christian Mission 6. Pretoria, South Africa: University of South Africa Press, 2000.
Anderson, Ray S. *Ministry on the Fireline: A Practical Theology for an Empowered Church.* Downers Grove, IL: InterVarsity Press, 1993.
_____. *The Shape of Practical Theology: Empowering Ministry with Theological Praxis.* Downers Grove, IL: InterVarsity Press, 2001.
_____. (ed.). *Theological Foundations for Ministry: Selected Readings for a Theology of the Church in Ministry.* Grand Rapids: William B. Eerdmans Publishing Company, 1979.
Andrews, Dale P. *Practical Theology for Black Churches: Bridging Black Theology and African American Folk Religion.* Louisville: Westminster John Knox Press, 2002.
Bartleman, Frank. *Azusa Street.* Plainfield: Logos International, 1980.

Bass, Dorothy C. and Volf, Miroslav. *Practicing Theology: Beliefs and Practices in Christian Life.* Grand Rapids: William B. Eerdmans Publishing, 2001.

Bassett, William and Huizing, Peter (eds.). *Experience of the Spirit.* New York: The Seabury Press, 1974.

Beardslee, William (editor). *The Way Out Must Lead In: Life Histories in the Civil Rights Movement.* 2nd ed. Westport, CT: Lawrence Hill and Co, 1983.

Benvenuti, Sheri. "Pentecostal Women in Ministry: Where Do We Go from Here?" *Cyber Journal For Pentecostal-CharismaticResearch.* http://www.pctiiorg/cyberj/ cyberj1/ ben.html (accessed 14 January 2008).

Betz, Hans Dieter, *Galatians: A Commentary on Paul's Letter to the Churches in Galatia.* Philadelphia: Fortress Press, 1979.

Bloesch, Donald G. *The Holy Spirit: Works and Gifts, Christian Foundations, vol 5.* Downers Grove, IL: InterVarsity Press, 2000.

Blount, Brian K. *Can I Get A Witness? Reading Revelation through African American Culture.* Louisville: Westminster John Knox Press, 2005.

_____. *Cultural Interpretation: Reorienting New Testament Criticism.* Minneapolis: Augsburg Fortress Press, 1995.

Botha, Nico. "Metaphors and Portrayals of Jesus in New South African And Their Implications for Christian of Missiological Knowledge," *Mission is Crossing Frontiers: Essays in Honour of Bongani A. Mazibuko.* Pietermaritzburg, South Africa: Cluster Publications, 2003.

Braxton, Brad R. *No Longer Slaves: Galatians and African American Experience.* Collegeville: The Liturgical Press, 2002.

_____. "The Role of Ethnicity in the Social Location of I Corinthians 7:17-24." In *Yet with a Steady Beat: Contemporary U.S. Afrocentric Biblical Interpretation,* edited by Randall C. Bailey, 19-32. Atlanta: Society of Biblical Literature, 2003.

Bright, John, *The Authority of the Old Testament.* London: SCM Press, 1967.

Brown, Michael J. *Blackening of the Bible: The Aims of African American Biblical Scholarship.* New York: Trinity Press International, 2004.

_____. "The Libratory Savior." Lecture, Claflin University, Granville Hicks Leadership Academy, Orangeburg, SC, February 1, 2008.

_____. *What They Don't Tell You: A Survivor's Guide to Biblical Studies.* 1st ed. Louisville: Westminster John Knox, 2000.

Browning, Don S. *A Fundamental Practical Theology.* Minneapolis: Augsburg Fortress Press, 1991.

_____. *Practical Theology: The Emerging Field in Theology, Church, and World.* San Francisco: Harper & Row, 1983.

Brueggemann, Walter. *Biblical Perspectives on Evangelism: Living in a Three-Storied Universe.* Nashville, Abingdon Press, 1993.

Brumback, C. *What Meaneth This?* Springfield, MO: Gospel Publishing House, 1968.

Bruner, Frederick D. *The Doctrine and Experience of the Holy Spirit in the Pentecostal Movement and Correspondingly in the New Testament.* Los Angeles: Frederick Dale Bruner, Hamburg, 1963.

_____. *A Theology of the Holy Spirit: The Pentecostal Experience and the New Testament.* Grand Rapids: Eerdmans, 1970.
Budgen, Victor. *The Charismatics and the Word of God: A Biblical and Historical Perspective on the Charismatic Movement.* England: Evangelical Press, 1989.
Burgess, S.M. and G. B. McGee, G.B. (eds.), *Dictionary of Pentecostal and Charismatic Movements.* Grand Rapids: Zondervan Publishing House, 1988.
Butler, Anthea D. *Women in the Church of God in Christ: Making a Sanctified World.* Chapel Hill: University of North Carolina Press, 2007.
Cannon, Katie. *Katie's Canon: Womanism and the Soul of the Black Community.* New York: Continuum International Publishing Group, 1996.
Cartledge, Mark J. *Charismatic Glossalalia: An Empirical Study.* Burlington: Ashgate Publishing Company, 2002.
Cazden, Elizabeth. *Antoinette Brown Blackwell: A Biography.* Old Westbury, NY: Feminist Press, 1983.
Chan, Simon. *Pentecostal Theology and the Christian Spirit Tradition.* Sheffield, England: Sheffield Academic Press, 2000.
Christenson, Laurence. *Speaking in Tongues and Its Significance for the Church.* Minneapolis: Bethany House Publishers, 1968.
Chism, Keith A. *Christian Education for the African American Community.* Nashville: Discipleship Resources, 1995.
Clark, Mathew S. and Henry I. Lederle. *What is Distinctive about Pentecostal Theology?* Muckleneuk, Pretoria: University of South Africa, 1989.
Clines, D.J.A. "Biblical Hermeneutics in Theory and Practice," *Christian Brethren Review* 31, 32, 1982.
Coleman, Robert E. *Master Plan of Evangelism.* Grand Rapids: Fleming H. Revell/ Baker, 1993.
_____. *The Mind of the Master.* Wilmore: Christian Outreach, 2003.
_____. *Nothing to Do but to Save Souls,* Nappanee, IN: Evangel Publishing House, 1990.
_____. *The New Covenant.* Colorado Springs: NavPress, 1984.
_____. *The Master Plan of Evangelism,* Westwood, NJ: F.H. Revell, 1993.
Cone, James. *Black Theology and Black Power.* Mary Knoll: Orbis Books, 1997.
Conn, Charles W. *A Balanced Church.* Cleveland: Pathway Press, 1975.
Cooke, B. and G. Macy, (eds.). *A History of Women and Ordination V1: The Ordination of Women in a Medieval Context.* Lanham: The Scarecrow Press, Inc., 2002.
Cox, Harvey, *Fire from Heaven: The Rise of Pentecostal Spirituality and the Reshaping of Religion in the Twenty-first Century.* Reading, MA: Addison-Wesley Publishing Company, 1995.
_____. *The Future of Faith.* New York: HarperCollins, 2009.
Daniels, David D III., "'Doing All the Good We Can': The Political Witness of African American Holiness and Pentecostal Churches in the Post-Civil Rights Era," *In New Day Begun: African American Churches and Civic Cul-*

ture in Post-Civil Rights America, R. Drew Smith (ed.). Durham: Duke University Press, 2003.

_____. "The Cultural Renewal of Slave Religion: Charles P. Jones and the Emergence of the Holiness Movement in Mississippi." Ph.D. Dissertation, Union Theological Seminary, 1992.

Danker, Frederick W., Gingrich, F. Wilbur. *A Greek-English Lexicon of New Testament and Other Early Christian Literature.* Chicago: University of Chicago Press, 1979.

Dayton, Donald W. *Theological Roots of Pentecostalism.* Peabody, MA: Hendrickson Publishers, 1991.

Dempster, M. W., Klaus, B.D. and Petersen, D. (eds). *Globalization of Pentecostalism: A Religion Made to Travel.* Carlisle, CA: Regnum Books International, 1999.

Dempster, Murray A., Murray W. Dempster, and Byron Klaus. *Called and Empowered: Global Mission in Pentecostal Perspective.* Peabody, MA: Hendrickson Publishers, 1991.

DuBois, Ellen Carol, *Feminism and Suffrage: The Emergence of an Independent Women's Movement in America, 1848-1869,* (DuBois) Ithaca, Cornell University Press, 1978.

Dulles, Avery. *Models of the Church.* New York: Doubleday & Company, 1983.

Farley, Edward. *Ecclesial Reflection: An Anatomy of Theological Method.* Philadelphia: Fortress Press, 1982.

_____. *Theologia: The Fragmentation and Unity of Theological Education.* Philadelphia: Fortress Press, 1983.

Fee, Gordon D. *Listening to the Spirit in the Text.* Grand Rapids: William B. Eerdmans Publishing Co., 2000.

Felder, Cain Hope (ed.). *Stony the Road We Trod: African American Biblical Interpretation.* Minneapolis: Fortress Press, 1991.

Franklin, Robert Michael. *Crisis in the Village: Restoring Hope in African American Communities.* Minneapolis: Augsburg Fortress Press, 2007.

Gerloff, Roswith I. H. *A Plea for British Black Theologies: The Black Church Movement in Britain in its Transatlantic Cultural and Theological Interaction.* New York: Peter Lang, 1992, 2 volumes.

_____. (with Abraham Akrong)."Independents", contribution to the *Global Atlas*, Edinburgh Centenary 1910-2010. University of Edinburgh Press, 2009 (forthcoming).

_____."Pentecostals in the African Diaspora", in: A. H. Anderson and W. J. Hollenweger (eds.), *Pentecostals after a Century*, Sheffield: Sheffield Academic Press, 1999, 67-86.

_____."Theory and Practice of the Holy Spirit", in: *Ministries of the Holy Spirit*, Quaker Religious Thought 16/3, Rio Grande College, Ohio: Quaker Discussion Group, (Summer 1975), 2-17.

_____."Theological Education in Black and White: The Centre for Black and White Christian Partnership (1978-1985)", in: *Pentecost, Mission and Ecumenism, Essays on Intercultural Theology:* Festschrift in Honour of W. J. Hollenweger, Studies in the Intercultural History of Christianity No.75, Frankfurt a.M.: Peter Lang, 1992, 41-59.Gilbert, Oliver and Truth, Sojourner. *The Narrative of Sojourner Truth* (Kindle Edition). Old LandMark Publishing, 2006.

Gilkes, Cheryl Townsend. *If It Wasn't for the Women.* Mary Knoll: Orbis Books, 2001.

Gilkey, Langdon "The Spirit and the Discovery of Truth through Dialogue" *Experience of the Spirit* New York: Seabury Press, 1974.

Glass, Michael. "The New Testament and Circumcision." *Circumcision Information and Resource Pages* (October 2001). http://www.cirp.org/pages/ cultural/glass1/ (accessed 15 March, 2008).

Goff, James R, Jr. *Fields White unto Harvest: Charles F. Parham and the Missionary Origins of Pentecostalism.* Fayetteville: University of Arkansas Press, 1988.

Goheen, Michael. "The Urgency of Reading the Bible as One Story in the Twenty-first Century." Public lecture given at Regent College, Vancouver, B.C. Thursday, 2 November 2006.

Gordon, A. J. *The Ministry of the Spirit.* Philadelphia: American Baptist Publication Society, 1894.

Groome, Thomas. *Sharing Faith: A Comprehensive Approach to Religious Education and Pastoral Ministry – The Way for Shared Praxis.* New York: HarperCollins Publishers, 1991.

_____."Theology on Our Feet: A Revisionist Pedagogy for Healing the Gap between Academia and Ecclesia." *Formation and Reflection,* edited by Lewis Mudge and James Poling, 55-78. Philadelphia: Fortress Press, 1987.

Guder, Darrell L. *The Continuing Conversion of the Church.* Grand Rapids: William B. Eerdmans Publishing Co., 2000.

Hauerwas, Stanley and William H. Willimon. *Resident Aliens: Life in the Christian Colony.* Nashville: Abingdon, 1989.

Hayter, Mary, *The New Eve in Christ.* Grand Rapids: William B. Eerdmans Publishing Company, 1987.

Hewitt, Nancy A., *Women's Activism and Social Change, Rochester, New York, 1822-1872, (Hewitt)* Ithaca, Cornell University Press, 1984.

Hodges, Melvin, L. *The Indigenous Church.* Springfield, MO: Gospel Publishing House, 1976.

_____. *A Theology of the Church and Its Mission: A Pentecostal Perspective.* Springfield, MO: Gospel Publishing House, 1977.

Hodgson, Peter C. *Revisioning the Church: Ecclesial Freedom in the New Paradigm.* Philadelphia: Fortress Press, 1988.

Hollenweger, Walter J. *The Pentecostals.* Reprint, Peabody, MA: Hendrickson Publishers, 1988.

Holman, C.L. "Who is Spirit-Filled Anyway? Ephesians and Ecumenism (or Ecumenica Pneumatology)." *31st Annual Meeting of the Society for Pentecostal Studies.* November, 2002.

Hooker, Morna D. "The Letter to the Philippians," *The New Interpreter's Bible: A Commentary in Twelve Volumes.* Nashville: Abingdon Press, 2000.

Hough, Joseph C. Jr. and Cobb, John B, Jr. *Christian Identity and Theological Education.* Chico, CA: Scholars Press, 1985.

Hubner, Hans. *Law in Paul's Thought.* New York: Continuum International Publishing Group, 2004.

International Bulletin of Missionary Research. Vol. 30, No 2, April 2006.

Isasi-Diaz, Ada Maria. *Mujerista Theology: A Theology for the Twenty-first Century.* Mary Knoll: Orbis Books, 1996.

Israel, Adrienne M. *Amanda Berry Smith.* Lanham: Scarecrow Press, 1998.

Jacobsen, Douglas. Thinking in the Spirit: Theologies of the Early Pentecostal Movement. *Bloomington, IN: Indiana University Press, 2003.*

Jervell, Jacob. *Luke and the People of God: A New Look at Luke- Acts.* Minneapolis: Augsburg Publishing House, 1972.

Johnson, Alonzo. *Good news for the Disinherited: Howard Thurman on Jesus of Nazareth and Human Liberation.* Lanham: University Press of America, 1997.

Johnson, Luke Timothy. *The Acts of the Apostles: Sacra Pagina Series V5.* Collegeville: Liturgical Press, 1992.

Johnson, Todd M., "Three Waves of Christian Renewal: A 100-Year Snapshot," *International Bulletin of Missionary Research.* Vol. 30, No 2, April 2006.

Larson, David L. *The Evangelism Mandate: Recovering the Centrality of Gospel Preaching.* Wheaton: Crossway Books, 1992. Packer, J. I. *Evangelism and the Sovereignty of God.* Chicago: InterVarsity, 1961.

Lincoln, C. Eric and Lawrence H. Mamiya. *The Black Church in the African American Experience.* Durham: Duke University Press, 1990.

Luther, Martin, Johann Friedrich, Wilhelm Tischer, and Samuel Simon Schmucker. *A Commentary on St. Paul's Epistle to the Galatians.* Philadelphia: Quaker City Publishing House, 1872.

Madges, William and Michael Daley (eds.). *The Many Marks of the Church.* "The Acts of the Apostles and of the Holy Spirit: Pentecostal Reflections on the Church as Charismatic Fellowship," essay by Amos Yong. Mystic, CT: Twenty-Third Publications, 2005.

Maddox, Randy. *Responsible Grace: John Wesley's Practical Theology.* Nashville: Kingswood, 1994.

Maloney, David, M. *The Church Cannot Ordain Women to the Priesthood: Declaration of the Congregation for Doctrine of the Faith.* Chicago: Franciscan Herald Press, 1978.

Marsh, Charles. *The Beloved Community: How Faith Shapes Social Justice, from the Civil Rights Movement to Today.* New York: Basic Books, 2004.

Martin, David. *Pentecostalism: The World Their Parish.* Malden, MA: Blackwell Publishers, 2002.

Martin, Ralph P. *New Century Bible Commentary: Romans.* Grand Rapids: William B. Eerdmans Publishing Co, 1976.

Mason Temple Church of God in Christ. "We Shall Overcome: Historic Places of the Civil Rights Movement – Mason Temple Church of God in Christ." http://www. nps.gov/ nr/travel/civilrights/tn1.htm (accessed 27 December 2007).

Maxwell, David. *African Gifts of the Spirit: Pentecostalism and the Rise of a Zimbabwean Transnational Religious Movement.* Athens, OH: Ohio University Press, 2006.
Mazibuko, B.A., *Education in Mission/Mission in Education.* Frankfurt a.M.: Peter Lang, 1987.
McGee, Gary B. (ed.). *Initial Evidence: Historical and Biblical Perspectives on the Pentecostal Doctrine of Spirit Baptism.* Peabody, MA: Hendrickson Publishers, 1991.
McKim, Donald K. *Westminster Dictionary of Theological Terms.* Louisville: Westminster John Knox Press, 1996.
Metress, Christopher (ed), *Lynching of Emmett Till: A Documentary Narrative.* Charlottesville: University of Virginia Press, 2002.
Miller, Donald E. and James N. Poling. *Foundations for a Practical Theology of Ministry.* Nashville: Abingdon Press, 1985.
Miller, Donald E. and Jack L. Seymour. "Openings to God: Education and Theology in Dialogue." In *Theological Approaches to Christian Education,* Jack L. Seymour and Donald E. Miller (eds), 7-24. Nashville: Abingdon Press, 1990.
Mitchell, Ella P. (editor), *Women: To Preach or not to Preach.* Valley Forge, PA: Judson Press, 1991.
Niebuhr, H. Richard. *Christ and Culture.* San Francisco: HarperCollins, 2001.
Njoh, Ambe J., *Tradition, Culture and Development in Africa: Historical Lessons for Modern Development Planning.* Aldershot: Ashgate Publishing, 2006.
Ortloff, Hazel. *The Happiest People on Earth.* Old Tappan: Fleming H. Revell Company, 1975.
Paris, Arthur E. *Black Pentecostalism.* Amherst: The University of Massachusetts Press, 1982.
Poloma, Margaret M. "The Pentecostal Movement." Available from http://hirr.hartsem.edu/ research/ pentecostalism_ polomaart5.html (accessed 15 January 2008).
Randolph, David James. *The Renewal of Preaching.* Philadelphia: Fortress Press, 1969.
Rensburg, Gerhard van. comment on "The responsibility trap; African leadership model," The Gerhard van Rensburg Blog. http://neweraleadership.blogspot.com/2007/06/responsibility-trap-african-leadership.html (accessed 7 November 2008).
Robert, Dana. *Occupy Until I Come: A.T. Pierson and the Evangelization of the World.* Grand Rapids: William B. Eerdmans Publishing Co., 2003.
Russell, Letty M. *Christian Education in Mission.* Philadelphia: Westminster Press, 1967.
_____.*Church in the Round: Feminist Interpretation of the Church.* Louisville: Westminster/John Knox Press, 1993.

_____. *Growth in Partnership.* Philadelphia: Westminster Press, 1981.

_____. *The Future of Partnership*. Philadelphia: Westminster Press, 1979.

Sanders, Cheryl J. *Saints in Exile: The Holiness-Pentecostal Experience in African American Religion and Culture*. New York: Oxford University Press, 1996.

Sanneh, Lamin. O. *Translating the Message: The Missionary Impact on Culture*. Mary Knoll: Orbis Books, 1989.

Scheffers, Norman W. "The Biblical Imperative for Church Planting" *Africa Journal of Pentecostal Studies: Volume 2*. Hebron Theological College, December 2004.

Schüssler-Fiorenza, Elisabeth. *But She Said: Feminist Practices of Biblical Interpretation*. Boston: Beacon Press, 1992.

Scott John. *John Wesley's Conception and Use of Scripture*. Nashville: Abingdon Press, 1995.

Segundo, Juan Luis. *The Liberation of Theology*. Mary Knoll: Orbis Books, 1976.

Seven Assemblies of God Ministers. *The Pentecostal Pulpit*. Springfield, MO: Gospel Publishing House, 1964.

Singh, David Emmanuel, and Farr, Bernard C. (eds).*Christianity and Cultures: Shaping Christian Thinking in Context*. Carlisle, Cumbria: Regnum Books International, 2008.

Smail, T. A. *Reflected Glory: The Spirit in Christ and Christians*. London: Hodder and Stoughton, 1975.

Smith, Amanda Berry. *Autobiography: The Story of the Lord's Dealings with Mrs.Amanda Smith, the Colored Evangelist.*1893. Chicago: Afro-American Press, Division of Afro-American Books, Inc., 1969.

Snyder, Howard A. *Liberating the Church*. Downers Grove: InterVarsity Press, 1983.

Spong, John Shelby. *Why Christianity Must Change or Die: A Bishop Speaks to Believers in Exile*. San Francisco: HarperCollins, 1999.

Stark, Rodney. "A Taxonomy of Religious Experience", *Journal for the Scientific Study of Religion* (5) (1965).

Strong, James, *A Concise Dictionary of the Words in the Greek Testament: With their Renderings in the Authorized English Version*. Nashville: Thomas Nelson Publishers, 1990.

Swete, Henry B. *The Holy Spirit in the New Testament*. London: McMillan, 1909.

Synan, Vinson. *The Holiness-Pentecostal Tradition: Charismatic Movements of the Twentieth Century*. Grand Rapids: William B. Eerdmans Publishing Co, 1997.

Tanner, Kathryn. *Theories of Culture: A New Agenda for Theology*. Minneapolis: Augsburg Fortress Press, 1997.

Thurman, Howard. *Jesus and the Disinherited*. New York: Abingdon-Cokesbury Press, 1949.

_____. *The Search for Common Ground: An Inquiry into the Basis of Man's Experience of Community.* Richmond, IN: Friends United Press, 1986.
Tillard, Jean. *Flesh of the Church, Flesh of Christ.* Collegeville, MN: Liturgical Press, 2001.
Tillich, Paul. *Theology and Culture.* New York: Oxford Press, 1959.
Trulear, Harold Dean. "Ida B. Robinson: The Mother as Symbolic Presence",James R. Goff and Grant Wacker (editors), *Portraits of a Generation: Early Pentecostal Leader*s. Fayetteville: University of Arkansas Press, 2002, 309-323.
Tucker, David M. *Black Pastors and Leaders: Memphis 1819-1972.* Memphis: Memphis State University Press, 1975.
Turner, Max. *Baptism in the Holy Spirit. Grove Renewal Series.* Cambridge, MA: Grove Books, 2000.
Van der Van, Johannes. *Practical Theology: An Empirical Approach.* Kampen, Kok Pharos, 1993.
_____. *Education for Reflective Ministry.* Leuven: Peeters Publishers, 1998.
Veli-Matti, Karkkainen. *An Introduction to Ecclesiology: Ecumenical, Historical & Global Perspectives.* Downers Grove: InterVarsity Press, 2002.
_____.*Toward a Pneumatological Theology: Pentecostal and Ecumenical Perspectives on Ecclesiology, Soteriology, and Theology of Mission.* Lanham: University Press of America, 2002.
Vincent, Marvin R. *The International Critical Commentary: A Critical and Exegetical Commentary on the Epistles to the Philippians and to Philemon.* Edinburg: T&T Clark, 1955.
Wimberly, Edward P. *African American Pastoral Care.* Nashville: Abingdon Press, 1991.
White, Charles Edward. *The Beauty of Holiness: Phoebe Palmer as Theologian, Revivalist, Feminist, and Humanitarian* (Zondervan/Francis Asbury Press, 1986).
Williams, Deloros. *Sisters in the Wilderness: The Challenge of Womanist God-Talk.* Mary Knoll: Orbis Books, 1993.
Williams, Gwen. *A New Wave of Refreshing for the Nations' Kingdoms.* Bloomington, IN: Author House Publishing, 2006.
Wolfteich, Claire E. *Navigating New Terrain: Work and Women's Spiritual Lives.* New York: Paulist Press, 2002.
Yoder, John Howard. *Body Politics.* Nashville: Discipleship Resources Press, 1992.
Yong, Amos. *Beyond the Impasse: Toward a Pneumatological Theology of Religion.* Grand Rapids: Baker Academic, 2003.
_____. *Discerning the Spirit (s): A Pentecostal-Charismatic Contribution to Christian Theology of Religions.* Sheffield, England: Sheffield Academic Press, 2000.
_____. *The Spirit Poured Out on All Flesh: Pentecostalism and the Possibility of Global Theology.* Grand Rapids: Baker Academic, 2005.

Zikmund, Barbara Brown. *Discovering the Church*. Philadelphia: Westminster Press, 1983.

Zikmund, Barbara Brown, Adair T. Lummis, and Patricia M. Chang. *Clergy Woman: An Uphill Calling*. Louisville: Westminster John Knox Press, 1998.

Index

A

African American, 2, 9, 13, 17, 26, 29, 30, 31, 43, 50, 51, 53, 59, 60, 61, 63, 65, 66, 67, 68, 69, 70, 71, 78, 79, 82, 83, 85, 86, 94, 111
African Christian Diaspora Conference, 19, 62
African Diaspora, 13, 17, 19, 21, 35, 53, 62, 65, 66, 67, 71, 72, 73, 76, 92
Afrocentric, 59, 71
Akrong, 60
Akrong, Abraham, 49
Alexander, Estrelda, 71
Allen, Roland, 87, 94
Amanda Smith, 69, 79
Anderson, 14, 17, 21, 51, 58, 61, 87
Anderson, Allan, 39
Azusa Street Mission, 71

B

Baptism of the Spirit, 75
Baumfree, Isabella: Sojourner Truth, 68
Betz, 48, 60
Betz, Hans Dieter, 48
Bible, 9, 10, 28, 31, 36, 39, 48, 54, 55, 56, 57, 58, 59, 63, 64, 65, 66, 74, 77, 78, 79
Bible-based, 57, 58
Biblical interpretation: biblical interpretation, 10, 39, 64, 66
Biblical Interpretation, 59, 78
Black Church, 36, 50, 54, 60, 67, 70, 79
Blackwell, 14, 70, 79
Blackwell, Antoinette Brown, 70, 79
Blount, 78
Blount, Brian K., 65
Botha, 58, 78

Botha, Nico, 38
Braxton, 43, 44, 59
Braxton, Brad Ronnell, 16
Bright, 78
Bright, John, 66
Brown, 65, 66, 78, 79
Brown, Michael J., 16
Browning, 81, 86, 94
Browning, Don, 14
Bultmann, Rudolph, 54

C

Chloe, 67
Christian Education, 86, 94, 95
Christian theology, 36, 47, 57, 58, 72
church, 2, 9, 11, 13, 14, 17, 18, 19, 20, 21, 23, 24, 25, 26, 27, 28, 29, 30, 31, 32, 33, 34, 35, 36, 37, 38, 39, 40, 41, 42, 43, 45, 46, 47, 50, 51, 52, 53, 54, 55, 56, 57, 58, 59, 60, 62, 63, 64, 65, 66, 67, 68, 69, 70, 71, 72, 73, 74, 75, 76, 77, 78, 81, 82, 83, 및84, 85, 86, 87, 88, 89, 90, 91, 92, 93, 94
Church of God in Christ, 2, 31, 32, 51, 53, 60, 71, 85, 86
Church of God, Pillar of the Truth Church, 26, 31, 33, 34, 37, 38, 52, 82
Circumcision, 44, 60
Civil Rights Movement, 50, 51, 60, 85
Continued revelation, 43
Core Principles, 87
Cox, 14, 76, 80
Cox, Harvey, 16, 76
Cultural Imperialism, 67
culture, 2, 9, 10, 13, 17, 18, 19, 20, 24, 25, 26, 28, 29, 30, 34, 35, 37, 38, 39, 40, 41, 43, 44, 45, 46, 47, 48, 49, 50, 51, 52, 53, 54, 55, 56, 57, 58, 59, 62, 65, 66, 69, 72, 73, 74, 75, 76, 77, 80, 81, 86, 89, 90, 93
Culture, 29, 33, 37, 39, 40, 41, 43, 47, 49, 54, 55, 56, 57, 58, 59, 60, 61, 72, 78, 80, 94

D

Daniels, 51, 60, 85, 94
Daniels, David D., 51
Deborah, 66
Denominational polity, 18
Dialogue, 61, 87, 91, 92, 94
Doctrine, 80

E

Eastern societies, 52
Ecclesia, 94
Ecclesiology, 15
Esther, 66, 78
Euro-American denominations, 67
Eurocentrism, 10

F

Feminist, 64, 78, 79, 95
First Jerusalem Council, 46
Franklin, 61, 85, 94
Franklin, Robert M., 53

G

Gerloff, 16, 17, 21, 36, 49, 60
Gerloff, Roswith, 11, 49
Gilkey, 61, 72, 73, 80
Gilkey, Langdon, 56
Gilmore, 50
Gilmore, Thomas, 50
glossalalia, 27, 32, 58
Goheen, 49, 59
Goheen, Michael, 41
gospel, 2, 10, 13, 17, 18, 19, 20, 24, 32, 36, 37, 38, 39, 40, 41, 42, 43, 44, 45, 46, 47, 48, 49, 50, 51, 52, 53, 54, 55, 56, 57, 58, 59, 62, 64, 67, 68, 69, 70, 71, 72, 73, 75, 76, 77, 78, 80, 82, 84, 87, 90, 94
Gospel, 11, 39, 41, 49, 58, 61, 94
Greco-Roman, 40, 42, 45, 46, 88, 90
Groome, 40, 59, 81, 86, 91, 92, 93, 94, 95
Groome, Thomas, 10, 91

H

Hayter, 78
Hayter, Mary, 66
hermeneutic circle, 54, 55
hermeneutical lens, 73, 76
Hodges, Melvin, 87

Holy Spirit, 7, 8, 9, 13, 17, 18, 19, 20, 24, 25, 27, 28, 29, 32, 33, 35, 37, 39, 41, 45, 46, 50, 54, 55, 56, 57, 58, 59, 62, 64, 66, 67, 68, 69, 71, 72, 73, 74, 75, 76, 77, 80, 81, 85, 86, 87, 88, 89, 90, 92, 93
Hubner, 48, 60
Hubner, Hans, 48

I

Independent pentecostal churches: independent pentecostal churches, 13, 14, 16, 17, 20, 24, 25, 26, 31, 35, 38, 39, 44, 54, 66, 81, 82, 83, 84, 86, 87, 88, 89, 90, 92, 93
Isasi-Diaz, 67, 79
Isasi-Diaz, Ada Maria, 67

J

Jesus movement, 46
Jewish Christians, 46
John, 15, 53, 57, 58, 61, 73, 78, 79, 80, 85, 95
John, Cheryl Bridges, 82
Johnson, 23, 36, 45, 59
Johnson, Todd M., 23
Jones, 16, 60, 71
Jones, C. P., 51
Junia, 66

K

King, Martin Luther, 29
Koinonia: koinonia, 8, 89, 90

L

Language, 46
leadership, 9, 10, 18, 19, 20, 24, 25, 26, 27, 28, 35, 41, 57, 62, 65, 66, 68, 69, 70, 71, 72, 74, 75, 81, 82, 83, 85, 86, 87, 89, 90, 91, 92, 93, 94
liberating, 2, 9, 11, 13, 17, 18, 20, 24, 37, 38, 41, 43, 44, 48, 49, 50, 53, 59, 62, 64, 67, 71, 72, 74, 76, 77, 78, 81, 82, 86, 90
Luther, 30, 47, 48, 49, 58, 60
Luther, Martin, 63

M

Mason, 51, 60, 71, 86
Mason, Charles H., 51
Mazibuko, 38, 58, 78

Mazibuko, Bongani A., 37
Miriam, 66
Mt. Sinai Holy Church of America, 69

N

Neocharismatic, 23
Neo-pentecostals, 75
New Testament, 10, 27, 44, 45, 46, 54, 60, 65, 67, 76, 78, 95
Newberry, Warren B., 87, 94
Nico Botha, 78
Niebuhr, 40, 58
Niebuhr, H. Richard, 40
Njoh, 78
Njoh, Ambe J., 65
Non-Jews, 45

O

oppressed, 10, 38, 41, 50, 70, 71, 77, 85, 87
Ordination, 62

P

Palmer, 79
Palmer, Phoebe, 70, 79
Palmer, Walter, 70
Paloma, Margaret, 72
Participation, 91, 92
Partnership, 10, 16, 91, 95
Pastors: Pastor, 8, 15, 26, 27, 28, 32, 34, 36, 63, 69, 74, 83, 84, 88, 90
Paternalism, 87
Paul, 18, 37, 38, 41, 42, 43, 44, 45, 47, 48, 49, 50, 53, 55, 59, 60, 63, 64, 78, 80, 94
Peace Movement, 83
Pentecost, 45, 46, 76
Pentecostalism, 2, 14, 78, 80; pentecostalism, 10, 13, 19, 20, 24, 38, 51, 67, 71, 74, 76, 77, 80, 85
Pentecostal-type churches: pentecostal-type churches, 9, 13, 17, 18, 19, 20, 23, 24, 25, 27, 29, 35, 38, 39, 49, 51, 52, 53, 54, 56, 57, 63, 64, 65, 66, 67, 68, 72, 73, 74, 75, 77, 81, 84, 87, 88, 89, 93
People's Temple, 83
pneumatokos: pneumato, 87
Poloma, 80

Preaching, 53, 60

R

Randolph, 60
Randolph, David James, 50
Robinson, Ida Bell, 69
Rock of Life Church, 2, 21, 26, 27, 28, 29, 37, 54, 56, 80, 82, 92, 93
Russell, 91, 95
Russell, Letty, 82, 91

S

Sanneh, 41, 46, 49, 59, 60
Sanneh, Lamin, 10
Schüssler-Fiorenza, 78
Schüssler-Fiorenza, Elizabeth, 64
Scripture, 9, 10, 13, 18, 19, 20, 24, 25, 26, 28, 31, 32, 33, 35, 37, 38, 39, 43, 44, 45, 50, 52, 53, 54, 55, 56, 57, 59, 62, 63, 64, 65, 66, 73, 74, 75, 76, 77, 78, 80, 81, 86, 89, 93
Second Wave Renewal, 23
Segundo, 54, 55, 61, 78, 91
Segundo, Juan Luis, 54
Smith, 60, 68, 79, 94
Smith, Amanda, 68
Sojourner Truth, 68, 69, 79, 85
Spirit, 2, 8, 9, 10, 13, 17, 18, 20, 21, 23, 24, 28, 29, 32, 33, 35, 36, 37, 39, 41, 43, 45, 46, 50, 51, 54, 55, 56, 57, 58, 61, 62, 63, 67, 68, 71, 72, 73, 74, 75, 76, 77, 78, 80, 81, 82, 86, 87, 90, 92, 93
Spirit-filled, 13, 21, 23, 58, 68, 74, 80, 86, 93
Starks, Rodney, 72
Symbolic Reading, 76

T

Tanner, 57, 61
Tanner, Kathryn, 56
Third Wave Renewal, 23
Tillich, 80
Tillich, Paul, 72
Timotheus, 47
Titus, 36, 47, 48
Trilateral, 9, 68, 81; trilateral, 2, 17, 18, 19, 20, 35, 54, 62, 74, 77, 81, 82, 86, 88, 89, 90, 93

Trulear, 69

U

uncultural, 72
unilateral leadership, 18, 83, 91, 94
United House of Prayer for All People, 82, 83
United Pentecostal Church, 2, 26

V

Venn, Henry, 87

W

Way of Holiness, 70
Western Christianity, 54, 87
Western theology, 66
Williams, 31, 32, 34, 36
Williams, Delores, 65, 78
Womanist, 65, 78
women in ministry, 25, 33, 43, 74, 75
Word of God, 28, 38, 53, 66, 68, 71, 76, 78

Y

Yong, 76, 80
Yong, Amos, 15, 76

Scriptural Index

Gen 17:9-14, *46*
Deut 22:5, *33, 34*
Matt 28:19, *88*
Luke 4:18, *37, 77, 87*
Acts 2:1-13, *46*
Acts 2, 10, 12, 15, *44*
Acts 15, *2, 18, 47, 76*
Acts 16:3, *48*
Rom 3:1-4, *44*
I Cor 7:18-19, *44*
I Cor *43, 92*

I Cor 14:34, *43*
Gal 2:3, *48*
Gal 2:4, *44, 48*
Gal 2:15, *44*
Gal 3:28, *43, 92*
Phil 3:7-12, *41, 43*
Phil 3:14, *89*
Col 3:11, *43*
I Tim 1:15, *37, 38*
I Tim. 2:12, *43*
II Peter 1:20, *32*

www.ingramcontent.com/pod-product-compliance
Lightning Source LLC
Chambersburg PA
CBHW031713230426
43668CB00006B/203